HOW TO CHOOSE

A WRITING COACH

A Beginner's Guide

Ensuring your best chance

for publishing success

Ged Cusack

DISCLAIMER

This publication is designed to provide competent and reliable information regarding the subject matter covered. However, it is sold with the understanding that the author and the publisher are not engaged in rendering legal, financial or other professional advice. Laws and practices often vary from state to state and country to country and if legal or expert assistance is required, the services of a professional should be sought. The author and publisher specifically disclaim any liability that is incurred from the use or application of the contents of this book.

The publisher does not have any control over and does not assume any responsibility for author of third party websites and their content.

CONTENTS

Introduction

Although there are many reasons why people write, I am going to assume that if you are reading this book, you want to publish your writing. If you want to publish your writing, then I also assume that you want people to read it.

Writing successfully includes many aspects of the publishing process. From the first word that you type to the first time a reader opens your published book (and further), the use of a coach can help you along this journey.

Due to the internet and social media there are now so many coaches and specialists for us to choose from that just the idea of searching for the right coach can be overwhelming.

The objective of this book is to provide you a system to allow you to find the right coach, to give you the best chance of succeeding in writing.

Whether you are looking for a coach to help you to structure a sentence or to help you market your book on Amazon, this process can be used to achieve that goal.

Coaches' roles can vary depending on context but for the purpose of this book we are looking for someone who will hold you accountable, and provide resources to help further your abilities in the area of writing.

I have constantly thrown myself into new sports, business opportunities and other activities and I am always looking for ways to accelerate my learning process.

My preferred option in the past was to speed read between five and twenty samples of specific books from Amazon (usually in a day), then choose which books were most relevant and buy the full book for download. I would then speed read the full books and absorb the relevant information.

Even though I am a speed reader, I realized that there had to be a more efficient way to acquire new skills. I developed the system in this book so that I (and now you) can search out the most suitable specialists and coaches for the best possibility of success.

You may already have an internal process that helps you to decide some of the qualities that you would like in a coach. Following the system in this book will help you focus your processes and make them more efficient.

The cost of a coach's services and resources can be expensive in both time and money. You may pay several hundred to several thousand dollars or spend hundreds of hours following their system.

In order to get the best return on your investments of both time and money, I believe it is crucial to have criteria that will allow you to determine who to choose as a coach.

Although there may be lots of successful writing coaches out there, you will probably get the best results by predominantly using the services of just one at a time. This is not to say that you shouldn't look at the resources of other writing coaches, but if you want to mirror the success of someone, you should stick to their system as closely as possible.

A few statistics and why you need a coach

I'm a firm believer that the terms "Self-made man" and "Self-made woman" are inaccurate. Although certain individuals may have more drive to succeed than others, we all need support at various stages of our lives. Picture yourself as a baby, when you were first born. You couldn't have survived without the support of another human being.

Most have us have heard the saying that, "we all have a book inside of us". Whether you have already written your first book (or your second, or your third) or you are just starting out, the services of a coach should make your future writing journey much more fruitful.

If you are still thinking that you can probably make it on your own and can't see why you need a writing coach, I'd like to share some statistics with you. Although these statistics are only in relation to novels, most publishing has similar results in relation to individual writers.

In 2014 the website "Digitalbookworld.com" carried out a survey of over 9000 current and aspiring authors. The survey was in relation to authors' progress in writing their novels, including writing manuscripts and actual publication. Below are some of the results from that survey:

- Of the 9000 survey respondents, only approximately 58% had actually completed a manuscript. This number is slightly distorted as 33% of the group were already published authors.

- Of the 6000 respondents who were only classed as aspiring authors, only 36.7% had actually completed a manuscript.
- Only 23% of the 5220 survey respondents (who had completed their manuscript) had actually published their first book.

If we look at those figures we can see that with a roughly 60% chance of getting to the stage of completing a manuscript, you then have only a one in four probability of publishing it.

That means that the chances of you progressing from an idea to actually writing a book and getting it published is about 15%.

Although there may be various reasons why other writers don't publish their books, surely you want to have the best chance to beat those odds?

NB. The survey above only focused on authors getting to publication. When you look at book sales there are lots of different numbers bandied about but the most consistent I can find is that 93% of books sell 500 copies or less.

"The few who do are the envy of the many who only watch" –
Jim Rohn

How to use this book

This book is set out as a step by step process for you to follow, to help you choose a writing coach who suits your need.

The first chapter lays out the steps of the system and then the subsequent chapters detail each of the individual steps of the process.

Each of the chapters has exercises that build on the previous chapter. By completing these exercises in order you will create your own focused criteria for a coach and ultimately begin using their services.

I understand that there will be some readers who are more detail oriented than others, but I also realize that other readers may prefer to skim read their books. I have therefore included a consolidation of all of the exercises at the back of the book for your convenience.

By all means, use this book in whatever way best suits you but I would point out the importance of chapter two.

Please read chapter two and be specific about what you want from a coach. If you don't get focused on what you are trying to gain from a coach then you could waste a lot of valuable time looking in the wrong place.

However you decide to use this book, I urge you to remember that the point is to make your search for the most suitable coach as efficient as possible.

There is no time for procrastination, It's time for you to move on to chapter one!

*"The journey of a thousand miles begins with one step" – **Lao Tzu***

Chapter 1   The basic criteria for a writing coach

"I passionately believe in heroes, but I think the world has changed its criteria in determining who it describes as a hero" – **Richard Attenborough**

Basic Coach Criteria

Before we begin, I want to emphasize the differences between supporters and coaches. A supporter can be anyone, such as a family member or a business colleague, but not all of them could be classed as a coach.

A true coach doesn't just support you: they also provide guidance and hold you accountable to keep you on the course to achieve your goals.

In order for you to give yourself the best chance of success, you need a process and criteria that will allow you to compare potential coaches on a like-for-like basis.

Below is an overview of the process and criteria that we will be covering in the chapters in this book:

1. What do you want from a writing coach (The 5 phases to refining your answer)?

This part of the process is to determine what you want from a coach. It is broken down into five phases:

A. Asking the right questions.

- What do you want to achieve?
- Why do you want to achieve it?

B. Building a list of possibilities
- Listing all the coaching options you can think of to help you achieve this goal.

C. Confirming the priorities of your list
- Determining which option has the best potential for success can expedite your journey to your goals.

D. Determining to be focused
- Just because you know what your priorities are doesn't mean that is where your attention will stay.
- Having determined the best option for success, commit to focusing on this one option.

E. Executing the plan
- You know what you need so go out and find it.

N.B. Knowing what you want and focusing on that can keep you on target and expedite the whole process. This is one of the critical steps of the process.

2. Are you prepared to be coachable (held to account)?

Knowing what you are trying to achieve is great but one of the most important elements when choosing a coach is your own decision to be coachable.

I have friends and colleagues (and also versions of my former self) who say that they want to improve in a certain area but when they are challenged to be held to account, they profess that they can just hold themselves to account.

- When I was younger there were times that I believed I could pick most essential skills up by myself. Maturity has shown me that I can accelerate my learning by utilizing a coach and being coachable.
- If I ever find myself believing that a coach will not improve my learning results in a specific area (and that I can do it all myself) I ask myself the question, "How has that worked out for you so far?"
- If we truly want to achieve something and seek out a coach to help us succeed, then we must commit to being accountable to that coach.

Earlier on in my career as a business coach, some of my coaching clients seemed less interested in their own success than I did.

- Even though I was readily available and provided lots of support (including outside of standard business hours) they still struggled with being held to account.
- I made the mistake of helping some businesses based on a percentage of profit rather than for a set fee (so that I had some skin in the game) and this meant that the clients sometimes saw my work as free.
- I eventually added the lottery clause, to ensure that I wasn't totally out of pocket. The lottery clause meant that if a client won the lottery (or married into money etc.) and decided they no longer wanted to work on their business, there was some recompense for all of the work I had put in.

N.B. If you aren't prepared to be held to account then there is little point looking for a coach!

3. What is your current budget for a writing coach's services?

Before you research specific coaches it is important that you know what you have to offer this coach.

Although the cost of education can be seen as an investment you still need to look at the potential returns on that investment. There will usually be a balancing act between the financial or time costs that you are committing to a coach.

You need to ask yourself a few questions:

- What are the potential financial costs of using this writing coach's services?
- What are the potential time costs of using this writing coach's services?
- What are the potential sacrifices that you are prepared to make to achieve your goals?

4. What is your preferred style of learning?

One of our considerations when choosing how to use a coach is looking at what style of learning best suits us. Because most writers tend to be avid readers we may assume that they learn visually, this isn't guaranteed.

What learning style do you gravitate towards on the VAK (Visual, Auditory, and Kinesthetic) System?

In chapter eight we will look into this system in more detail but the core premise behind the VAK system is that we have a propensity to one of the following three styles of learning:

- Visual Learners   -   Learning best through visual stimulus

- Auditory Learners   -   Learning best when hearing information
- Kinesthetic Learners   -   Learning best through touching, feeling and doing

Of course this is only a guide and although it can help to make some learning more efficient, it is not effective in every situation. Trying to get better at basketball by listening to an audio book may not give you the same results as continuously throwing free throws.

Knowing your learning style may provide you some insight into how you would like to use a coach. It is only once you have searched for a coach and found what resources they have available that you can choose how you will best use them.

Points to consider:

- Even some of the world's top coaches provide one on one coaching (for the right price).
- If one of your decisions to seek out a coach is to hold you accountable, how accountable will you be just reading a coach's book or listening to their podcast?
- What resources does this coach provide? If the coach provides various courses or information, ensure you pick the right one for you.
- It could be that you find a classic book, such as "The Richest Man in Babylon" or "Think and Grow Rich" and determine that they will be your guide but most of us need more than that to achieve success in a specific area.

5. What are the main qualities you are looking for in a writing coach?

Although some of the most successful coaches may span multiple areas of writing, you need to prioritize the specific subject that you have determined is your focus.

- Is the potential coach a well-known writer in a specific field, to whom you look for inspiration?
- Do they excel in publishing a great volume of books in a short period of time?
- Are they well known for poetry or more mainstream writing pursuits?
- Have they actually coached anyone successfully already?
- Are they renowned for just one genre, such as teaching nonfiction, fantasy fiction, poetry etc?

You need to determine at what level this coach is currently operating in their specific area of knowledge.

- Do you want progressive coaches or just one for the whole journey (through to publication)?
- Can you leverage this coach's reputation in their area to attract other successful coaches on the next stage of your writing journey?
- Has this coach got the resources to help you on every step of your writing journey?
- Is this coach on their own journey of continual improvement or are they stuck at a set level?

Are they an ethical person?

- This is an essential quality if you are going to be adopting their processes and style
- You may not have comprehensive information on a coach but trust your instincts here

6.   Researching and finding your coach.

Now that you have examined what you have to offer and determined what you want from a coach, it is time to start your search.

Online searches are usually the first thing we contemplate in the modern age and as this is one of the most common methods of research. Here are a few options:

- Google searches
- Facebook groups
- LinkedIn
- Amazon.com

Referrals can also be a good place to start to look for a writing coach. Consider:

- Have you got friends who are currently using a writing coach?
- Have you recently heard a coach mentioned at an event or on social media?

If you have previously used a coach for another subject, would they be suitable in this stage of your writing journey?

- If the answer is yes, for what purpose did you use them previously?
- The reason you may not consider previous coaches first is that your current search may not be in their area of expertise.

- If you came across two coaches for a specific subject, the fact that you have already used the resources of one of them may affect your choice of a coach.
- Dependent on your previous results, with this coach, it may actually sway your choice against them for this new subject.

N.B. Don't feel obligated to choose a coach because of a referral or because you have used them previously. Run them through your research process and if the results show that they are as suitable as their competition then you may use your familiarity to tip the balance in their favour. Remember your primary goal is to choose a coach who will provide the most benefit for you!

7. Confirming how you will use your coach

Once you've gone through the book and completed the exercises, the previous steps in this process will have created a shortlist of potential coaches (you may have narrowed it down to just one coach). Taking into account all of the previous factors, such as your budget and style of learning etc., you next need to determine how you will best use the services of this coach.

- One on one coaching (either directly with the coach or through the team of a coach) is usually seen as one of the most effective forms of coaching. This can also be the most expensive.
- Following along with a coach's teachings via books or on free YouTube videos may cost less cash but can be more time intensive (and less effective at keeping you on track).
- Perhaps you are looking at a hybrid of the two previous options – some kind of course but limited feedback.

This is where the rubber meets the road and by the end of this stage you should have a coach.

Although this may be seen as the final step in the process, you may need to modify your plan once you start to use a coach. Remember you don't know what you don't know, so remain flexible.

N.B. It may be uncomfortable to admit this but when you attempt to make a change in any area of your life, some of your supporters (friends or family) may not support you in this change. It doesn't mean that they don't want to support you – in many cases they are just concerned that you are setting yourself up to fail.

Whether you are hoping to write for a living or just want to write the one novel (that we believe we all have inside us), supporters may think that they are saving you from embarrassment.

The decision to make a change can create added stress to our lives. In order to avoid adding extra stress when you start out on a new journey, I suggest you limit whom you initially inform that you are committing to this journey.

Chapter 2   The five phases to determining your goal

Before we start to search for a coach, we need to determine what we are trying to achieve (our goal). You may be looking for a coach to help you in various areas of your life but you need to prioritize those areas. Once you've determined where to focus, you can then look for a coach who provides you the best return on your investment (ROI) in that particular area.

In this chapter we are going to work through a process to allow you to determine the primary goal that you are wanting to achieve with a coach.

In-depth goal setting can be very time consuming – in fact there are whole books and courses on that subject. I am assuming that by reading this book you already have some inkling of an area where you require the assistance of a coach. For this chapter we are just going to focus on the basics to allow you to refine what you primarily want to gain from a coach.

*"The question you should be asking isn't, "What do I want?" or "What are my goals?" but "What would excite me?" — **Tim Ferris***

The Five Phases

A. Phase 1   =   Ask the right questions

1. What do you want to achieve (your goal)?

Before you start to search for the services of a coach you need to determine what you are trying to achieve. If you don't get this right, it may result in you hiring a coach who is not fit for your purpose. Be specific here and aim to describe what you want (that will spark your fire) in just one sentence.

Some suggestions:
- I want to be the highest paid science fiction writer in the world.
- I want to build a six figure business by writing science fiction.
- I want to write bedtime stories for my children.
- I want income from book royalties to be triple the amount of my government pension.
- I want to produce a business book to supplement my coaching services.

2. What specific area of the writing process do you want assistance from this coach?

Some suggestions:
- I want a coach to help me with my life's vision before I approach any writing.
- I need help with the basic structure of the creative writing process.
- I already have a manuscript but need someone to take me through the editing phase.
- I have self-published a book already but need someone to help me produce sales.
- I am a successful nonfiction writer who needs help transitioning to writing fiction.

3.   What degree of success do you want to achieve?

Once you have decided on the specific subject area of writing that you want help with, you need to define what degree of success you want a coach to help you achieve. This can be an ultimate goal or an interim goal (depending on how far you wish to go).

Some suggestions:
- I want to build a six figure business by writing thrillers.
- I want to create enough income from book royalties to double the amount of my current government pension.
- I want to write six picture books for my children.
- I want to write to express myself creatively.
- I want to turn my current six manuscripts into published novels.

N.B. Knowing what you want and at what level you are aiming for can also help you determine whether a coach is suitable for you.

4.   Why do you want to achieve this writing goal?

In any endeavour there will be times that challenge you. If you don't know why you are doing it you may struggle to complete that endeavour.

Some suggestions:
- I cannot survive on my current pension and no one will employ someone of my age.
- I want to tell the story of my family before I die.
- I want to create an amazing experience for my children that they will remember for the rest of their lives.

B. Phase 2   =   Build a list of possibilities
There are more than likely several possible ways to achieve your goal.
- Listing more than one alternative allows you to consider other options.
- Opening your mind to alternatives can mean that you find more efficient ways to proceed.

C. Phase 3   =   Confirm priorities
Prioritize your list:
- The smaller the list the easier it may be to prioritize.
- However big your list is you need to determine your priorities in order to be efficient with your resources.

D. Phase 4   =   Determine to focus on your goal
Just because you know what your priorities are doesn't mean that is where your attention will stay:
- Keeping a laser focus on your goal will help you focus the majority of your resources there.
- Focus helps you reduce distractions so you need to commit to staying focused on your priorities.

E. Phase 5   =   Execute the plan
Reading books and writing plans can only get you so far:
- It's said that success is 10% inspiration and 90% perspiration so you need to take action.
- Having a plan in place can mean that you reduce the amount of perspiration that you waste.

- By now you have determined exactly what you need and committed to focusing on that need. It's time to take action.

My initial use of coaches

When I started my own personal development journey over two decades ago I had heard of the likes of Anthony Robbins etc. but I wasn't focused on what I was trying to achieve.

One of the first books I read was Robert Kiyosaki's "Rich Dad Poor Dad" and in the following months I bought all of his books and his "Cashflow game". Not all of his books were relevant to me at that time but when you aren't sure what you are searching for, you can get distracted.

Today I am more selective with my choice of coaches and resources but it was only by learning from my mistakes that I realized I need to be precise in my searches.

In order to determine exactly what you require from a coach, you need to keep asking questions and drill down to find your goal.

Although all of the steps of this process are important, I have provided a short case study below for only the first three phases to give you extra guidance on these core steps.

The three phases to choosing what you want

The first three phases are the primary process to determining how to proceed, so the exercises in this chapter only focus on those first three phases.

It may initially seem obvious what you need from a coach but the fact that "We don't know what we don't know" means that we might need to ask the same question a few times to get the real answer.

Phase four and five are relatively straight forward:

- Confirm what you want.
- Do something about it.

The case study will assist you in completing these exercises. You will find the complete study in Chapter 9, but I have provided a short extract here to get you started.

Case Study

Martin is a fifty year old business coach who has been successfully coaching individuals for years. He knows that his knowledge and experience could benefit a lot more clients if he were to condense his training systems into a book.

A. What does Martin want to achieve?
- Martin wants to write a business book that encompasses his teaching systems and provides a resource for business owners.

B. Why did Martin want to do this?
- He wants to expand the amount of clients that he can service with his expertise.

C. Martin's list of possibilities to achieve the writing and publication of this book
- Employ a ghost writer and just slap his name on the book.
- Muddle through writing the book himself and hope that he can finish it.

- Employ a writing coach who has been successful in publishing business books.
- Employ a writing coach who is successful in helping clients produce their own business books and self-publish.
- Hire an experienced proposal writer and then complete the book himself to pitch to a publishing house.
- Buy several books on "how to write a book" and work through their exercises.

D. Martins prioritized list

Option	Priority
Employ a ghost writer and just slap his name on the book.	4
Muddle through writing the book himself and hope that he can finish it.	6
Employ a writing coach who has been successful in publishing business books.	2
Employ a writing coach who is successful in helping clients to produce their own business books and self-publish.	1
Hire an experienced proposal writer and then complete the book himself.	5
Buy several books on "how to write a book" and work through their exercises.	3

Exercises

Exercise One   What are you trying to achieve?
Determine what you are trying to achieve and write this in a one sentence statement e.g.

- I want to supplement my business coaching services by writing a book in my field.
- I want to publish my first novel.
- I want to build a long term career as an author.

Exercise Two   Determine your Why
Determine why you want to achieve this and write this in a one sentence statement e.g.

- I want to be in charge of my own financial destiny.
- I want to tell the story of my family before I die.

Exercise Three   Compile your list
Write a list of options to achieve this goal (up to ten but a minimum of three) to allow you to focus on the solutions for your goal.

However you have compiled your list (spreadsheet, word document etc.) a table is one of the best options. You only need two columns for this table.

- List all of your options in the left hand column of the table.
- Write freely and don't worry how "outside of the box" these ideas seem.
- The main thing here is to just compile your list.

Exercise Four   Prioritize your list
Once you have completed the last exercise you should now have a table with the left hand column full of options to achieve your goal and the right hand column empty.

Now to prioritize:

- In the right hand column allocate a number against each option based on how likely this option is to help you achieve your goal.
- Allocating the number "one" for the option with the highest probability for success, then number "two" for the next highest probability, and so on and so on.

24

Chapter 3   Being accountable

I have to confess from the outset that I like to be my own boss. As someone who spent twenty two years in the British Military it surprises some people when I say, "I don't like being told what to do."

Like many people, the thought of being accountable to somebody else can seem uncomfortable to me.

Before we go any further in this chapter I want to reiterate the difference between a supporter and a coach (as stated earlier in this book).

A supporter just provides support but a coach provides support and holds you accountable!

"Accountability breeds response-ability" — **Stephen R Covey**

In this chapter we are going to look at different options for accountability and I will describe to you some of my own experiences with accountability to coaches.

Although there are various ways in which you can be held accountable by a coach, these can be classified into the following two categories:

- Contact with the coach (or their team).
- No contact with the coach (or their team).

Contact   -   One on One / Team on One Accountability

The term "one on one" implies that there are only two people in the relationship but as lots of successful coaches have teams to provide feedback and guidance, I include "team on one" under the same heading.

I have personally employed one on one coaches in various areas of my business and social life over the years and there have been times when, prior to an upcoming (weekly or monthly) coaching session, I knew that I hadn't taken enough action between sessions.

One thing I have learnt is that it is best to be honest about these omissions – to maintain the integrity of your relationship with your coach.

My experience: Foreign Exchange Trading

When I first started using a coach for Foreign exchange (Forex) trading, I had already been trading stock options and other financial products for several years.

I sought out someone who I knew was a successful trader and approached him for one on one coaching.

One of the issues with using any kind of financial trading coach is that there can still be occasions where you will lose money, even though you are following their guidance. Unfortunately financial markets are not always logical and if you can't take a loss you shouldn't be trading. The psychology of continuing to trade after losing money can add even more stress to your psyche and you have to dig deep to maintain the agreements that you established with your coach.

My one on one sessions tended to be monthly and this meant that I had to remain self-motivated during the period in between sessions.

I was committed to keeping to a schedule but there were times over the length of the coaching training (of two to three years) that I was unwell, which sometimes meant I had missed a quarter of the trading sessions for that month.

I notified my coach in advance of our session and we sometimes (only rarely) postponed; but on most of the occasions we kept to our scheduled session and I still got lots of benefits by attending.

The coaching relationship is not just about a rigid schedule of training but also the knowledge that a good coach is there for your support. You need to be accountable but also honest.

My experience: Martial Arts
When I first started learning Wing Chun I was coached in a one on one weekly session for three hours. I would do my best to train every day (in between the sessions) but sometimes other activities would seem more important.

My lack of training in between some training sessions was a disadvantage to me when I attended those coaching sessions. This realization drove me to reaffirm my commitment to being held accountable.

I use this example because my lack of training resulted in physical pain when I attended the sessions. Your writing omissions may not result in your coach inflicting physical pain on you, but the psychological damage that you can inflict on yourself may be worse (and longer lasting) than any physical pain.

No Contact   -   Book / Course Accountability
Following a book or online course for coaching means that you are committing to be accountable to this course. This usually

means that only your personal willpower and individual integrity will maintain your accountability.

In Brian Cohen's book "How to Write a Sizzling Synopsis" (a book that provides some great advice for writers trying to produce shorter descriptions of their books) he mentions in his first chapter that he would like to guilt the readers into completing all of the exercises in his book. He is trying to hold the readers accountable so that they can get the most benefit from his book.

Over the years I have followed many courses and worked through many, many exercises in books. One of the benefits of following a set course is that they allow you to learn at your own pace. If we are the type of person who binge watches TV series we may try to condense our learning timetable and binge learn.

Not all courses suit binge learning because if a resource is designed to build habits, you are required to repeat certain activities over a continuous period in order to build that habit.

You may find that a writing coach requires you to produce a set amount of writing or to write for a set amount of time each day. Below are a few examples of my own attempts at accountability with this kind of coaching.

Wealth Training

One of the coaches I have used over the years is Paul McKenna. I like his way of teaching and of his resources that I have used, I particularly enjoyed working through his book, "I can Make You rich".

Several of the exercises in this book require some time commitment, including:

- Listening to the Hypnosis Audio (for approximately twenty five minutes) each day.
- Writing ten answers to the wealth questions, every day for thirty days.

The book includes many other daily and more regular activities and I have to admit that I have not always been able to complete these exercises every day.

Because you may be setting your own timetable here I think it is important to determine what is realistic.

If you choose to do the thirty day exercise in five day chunks (taking the weekends off) you may not get the same results but at least by still setting a timetable you are holding yourself accountable.

Manifestation Meditation

Another coach I have used several times is Wayne Dyer. Of all of his books and resources that I have used, I particularly like his audio meditations for manifestation.

Although this might not seem specific to writing, I'm a firm believer that mind-set is very important to writers.

This might seem like a simple concept of working with the audio but I was committing to doing this regularly:

- Every morning when I awoke.
- Every night before I went to sleep.

Carrying out certain activities (such as brushing your teeth) every morning and night may come naturally to you. The thing to note is those habits have probably been developed over years or decades and starting new habits can be a challenge.

Whenever I have worked through Wayne Dyers' exercises I have had to prioritize over other activities, e.g. I couldn't do other audio hypnosis exercises at the same time.

Some people may class me as having a "steadfast determination" about me, because I tend to display distinct focus when I'm working on a subject. Even I sometimes miss the odd session in a program that requires continuous input.

Creative Writing

In my journey to becoming a fiction writer I realized that I had to polish my creative writing skills.

I purchased a book with fifty creative writing exercises and committed to completing all of the exercises in this book within two months.

So my time commitment here was:

- Complete fifty creative writing exercises (ranging from 500-1000 words).
- Complete one exercise a day. With a two month deadline this allowed me a 20% time contingency to allow for distractions.

Various things happened (including a death in the family) and six months later I had only completed two of the exercises.

It was clearly not a priority or I would have found the time. This is where a strong reason – a "Why" – would have helped me.

Justifying not being accountable

"He that is good for making excuses is seldom good for anything else" — **Benjamin Franklin**

Although we may start off with good intentions on day one of our training under a coach, as we progress there are many justifications that we use to break our accountability agreements.

Below are just some of the excuses that we use to justify our lack of action:

- It's okay, my one on one coach will never know what I've been doing.
- If I miss a day of training I can always do twice as much tomorrow.
- I'm not seeing any results yet so what's the point in sticking to this stupid schedule?
- Twenty one days is such a long time, the coach can't expect me to do this every day.
- I have more important things to do with my time.
- I didn't realize how much work this would involve.
- My friends and family say this is a waste of time so why am I bothering?

If you carry out a thorough process of determining what you want to achieve and know what commitment this will entail, then you should look at excuses as a test of your own integrity.

"The four most expensive words in the English language are, 'This time it's different" — **Sir John Templeton**

Being Realistic

If you have a strong enough reason to want to achieve your goal, it will make it easier to ignore the voice in your head that is telling you, you can continue to break your agreement with your coach (and still achieve your goals).

I will discuss your time budget in the next chapter but I urge you to be realistic in your commitments, as this will make it so much easier to stay the course.

Exercises

I believe that accountability is a state of mind and requires us to make the decision to be accountable. In order to examine this state of mind further, I have formulated a few exercises below.

Before you start to consider committing to a coach I want you to work through these three exercises and start to focus on your accountability.

Exercise Five   Historical accountability

Most of us have been accountable in some shape or form in our past but we can't always recount those situations.

In this exercise, I want you to list any time in the past when you have either been accountable to someone else or held yourself accountable. This doesn't have to be anything major, I just want you to remember that you have previously been accountable for something.

Below are a few general suggestions:

- Studying for exams. This can relate to any level of education as there are always potential distractions.

- Completing your school homework. As children there are ways and means to avoid homework but if you completed it regularly, you held yourself accountable.
- Saving money to purchase something. This could be something that you saved for as a child or perhaps a deposit for a car or house later in life.
- Adhering to a curfew that you had to be home by as a child.
- Completing exercises in your own time (with no supervision) as set by a sports coach.
- Practising a musical instrument or dance routine for a performance.

The suggestions above are just a few general examples and most people can relate to at least one of them. Feel free to use any of these examples or recount an instance more relevant to your own experience.

Exercise Six   **Rating your success**

Once you have recounted several times when you have been accountable, I want you to rate those instances of accountability.

- Rate the success of your results on a scale of zero to five (with zero being total failure and five being total success).
- If you rate any results at a three or above then those situations can be classed as being successful in holding yourself to account.
- If you rate any results at a two or below then those situations can be classed as being unsuccessful in holding yourself to account.
- Try to remember at least one time where your accountability provided a successful outcome and another where it did not.

If you can't remember any time that your accountability resulted in a successful outcome, it doesn't mean that you aren't coachable. You may just need to be extra steadfast when making your new commitments.

If you can't remember any time that your accountability resulted in a failed outcome that doesn't mean that you don't need a coach. You just might have an advantage in maintaining the coaching agreement.

Exercise Seven   **Checking your current accountability**
The previous two exercises were designed to help you focus on an accountability frame of mind. Whatever your previous results, they don't dictate your future success or otherwise.

In order to refresh your mental state and prove that you can hold yourself to account, I want you to undertake the following exercise:

- For the next seven days, record the statement "I (insert your name) am willing to be coachable".
- You can choose to use a voice recorder, write in a notebook or make a note on your smartphone.
- You choose a specific time that is suitable to you (if it would help, set an alarm on your phone or in your calendar).
- I want you to record this at the same time for seven days because this time period will span a weekend. Most people who plan their weekdays around work don't hold themselves to the same standards at weekends.

N.B. Once you start to use a coach there may be circumstances that will challenge your agreement to be accountable to your coach. By completing the simple exercise above, you are making a commitment to me and you. If you have trouble completing this exercise the first time, start again for a different seven day period.

A strong reason for what you are doing will help to keep you accountable.

36

Chapter 4   Determining your budget

When we hear the word "budget" most of us think purely about money, but for many people the amount of time we have available is more important than the amount of money.

Whatever we are hoping to achieve with the help of our coach, we will be investing either more time or more money, and whichever of these valuable resources we are committing we want the optimum return on our investment.

The cost of a coach's services can range from a couple of hundred to several thousand dollars in financial commitment, and you could potentially be committing hundreds of hours to following a coach's system. I believe it is essential to consider what your budget is going to be for this project, factoring in time as well as money, and also considering the opportunity costs.

The Opportunity costs

For those of you who have read some of my other books, you will have seen that I go in depth into the concept of opportunity cost there. For the purpose of this chapter I will summarize it in a few bullet points.

- When we are investing our time or money into an opportunity, we are aiming for a return on that investment.
- By committing our resource (of either time or money) we are limiting our ability to invest that resource in another opportunity.
- If we invest our resource wisely then the return on that investment can be beneficial to us but if we do not receive a reasonable return on our investment (ROI), this comes at a cost.

- The cost is the difference between our actual returns from our investment and the potential returns that we could have received had we invested our resource in another opportunity.

By optimizing your investment you reduce your opportunity cost.

The main reason we choose to look for a coach is to expedite our results. Direct access to a coach can speed up our progress substantially more than just reading their books.

The amount of time or money you have available (your budget) can determine how you can utilize a coach.

The majority of people see themselves as having a limited amount of cash to invest in a coach and this can result in false economy with limited results.

"If you're serious about changing your life, you'll find a way. If you're not, you'll find an excuse" — **Jen Sincero**

Jen Sincero is a #1 New York Times bestselling author and success coach. In her book "You are a Badass" she talks about the time she invested in her own success coach when she was financially broke. After paying for the coach's services with her credit card she had a case of buyer's remorse and asked the coach to refund the money. Luckily the coach talked her into continuing with the coaching and Jen credits this decision with being one of the reasons for her success.

After hiring her first coach she actually tripled her income within six months!

Financial Budgets

When I left the corporate world and decided to pursue e-commerce, I made sure that I had a certain amount of savings as a financial safety net. I had determined that some of these savings would be allocated to my education in this field.

Whatever your reason for looking for a writing coach, there is a high probability of there being some financial costs.

The spectrum of this cost can be huge:

- A one on one coaching session with someone like Seth Godin or Anthony Robbins (if they accept you) can cost millions of dollars.
- The cost of a digital book or an online course can actually start at $0.00.

With such a disparity between potential costs you can see that you need to know what your financial education budget is.

Before you determine how much you are going to allocate to education in this subject (a large percentage of which will include paying for the coach's resources) I want you to consider a few questions:

A. How much can you afford to spend without it affecting your ability to cover your normal expenses?
- Although you may feel that the importance of following your passion is your highest priority, you will need to determine what amount you can afford to commit to this coaching.

- Coaching fees can be serviced via ongoing payments rather than just a one off payment. This doesn't mean that you are paying any less overall and needs to be balanced with your long term financial plans.

B. What is the potential return on your financial investment in this subject?

- I understand that it can be hard to quantify the potential financial impact on your writing career from activities such as improving your creative writing skills or storytelling ability. If a coach helps you write a novel you have no idea if it will be a bestseller or not.

- Although it might be true that if a coach allows you to achieve life changing results in any area of your writing life, you are getting a good return on your investment, you may be after more quantifiable financial results.

- If you are investing in a writing coach as a means to improve your financial situation, I would suggest that the financial benefits of the coaching need to actually cover the financial cost of the coaching. The financial results may not be immediately apparent but you should be able to get some idea from any coach who requires a large financial investment.

- You need to realize that there may be no financial return on your investment but a good coach should identify that there are no guarantees. For this reason, do not commit funds that you cannot afford to lose.

C. Does the coach offer a money back guarantee?

- Reputable coaches and organisations usually offer a money back period ranging from 30 to 90 days for you to determine if your investment was justified.

- Ensure that you use any of these refunds if you feel that you have not received what you paid for, as this can free up funds for you to purchase the right resource.

Financial Exercises

Exercise Eight   Spending

In this exercise I want you to determine how much discretionary spending money you have available to commit to a writing coach.

As most of us make our payments digitally nowadays, it can be relatively easy to look back over our bank and credit card statements to track our spending.

You need to list where you allocate of your income. Use the four categories below to help you list your expenditure:

A. Household Expenses
- List all of your monthly expenses (rent, mortgage, utilities, fuel etc.).

B. Business Expenses
- This may be easy to calculate: if you don't currently run a business it should be zero.

C. Savings
- You may have automated savings coming out of your income.
- As compound interest works best when you start to save early, I recommend that you continue contributing to your savings.

D. Discretionary Spending
- This includes any social spending but also any expenses that can be reduced.
- If you have a mobile phone plan or a cable TV package, can you reduce these costs?
- If you have credit card payments, can you negotiate to get the payments reduced?

N.B. The sum total of all of these figures should total your income. If not go back and check your figures.

Exercise Nine   **Financial Commitments**

Now that you have determined where you spend your money, you need to determine how much of your discretionary spending you are willing to commit to your writing coach.

Just because you have an amount of funds available, that does not mean you should commit it all. Although you may be able to estimate the financial benefits of using this coach there are no 100% certainties in your ROI.

Before you commit any finances, you need to decide what the total loss of this money with no financial benefits would mean to you.

Paying for a coach with your credit card with the hope that the financial returns a coach provides will pay off this credit card is not advisable.

*"Only a moron starts a business on a loan" – **Mark Cuban***

This quote from Mark Cuban may seem to reinforce the idea that you shouldn't use your credit cards to start a business. As Mark actually borrowed $15,000 to start his first business it may disprove this fact. The main point is that any business expense (including hiring a coach) needs to be critically assessed.

If you discovered in the last exercise that you don't have any discretionary funds available, you may need to create some extra income.

Decide how much money you are willing to commit and commit it:

- Only you can determine what amount of money you are willing to risk here.
- Confirm your amount, write it down and commit that you are allocating these funds.

Time Exercises

With a never-ending list of demands on our time we are constantly having to prioritize how we spend that time.

"Nobody ever sat on their death be and said, 'I wish I'd spent more time at the office' " — ***anonymous***

When people consider an investment in a coach, they usually primarily think of the financial costs and focus less on the time requirements.

In order to draw your attention to the time requirements of employing a coach, I want you to ask yourself a couple of questions:

- How much time do you have available outside your normal income-generating and sleep activities? Income generation can refer to immediate as well as long term income streams. Remember that some amount of sleep is essential to our physical wellbeing.
- How much time are you willing to commit to your coaching training?

Although you may feel there isn't enough time in a day, if you analyze where you spend your time, you may be surprised.

Exercise Ten　　　　**Time monitoring**

For this exercise, divide the next seven days into 15 minutes segments and log where you spend that time.

You can choose to track this in a spreadsheet or in a notebook but I encourage you to update this log as often as possible. There are productivity apps (such as "Focus Keeper) that allow you to set a timer for a 15 minute period. Use one of these if it helps you.

If you choose to list your activities at the end of each day (rather than regularly updating your log during the day) you may find it hard to remember how much time you devoted to each activity.

Rather than trying to classify time into lots of different categories, I find that just using the following five categories works best for me:

1. Work:　　　This relates to any income-generating activity.

2. Travel: This relates to travel to and from work so if you work from home this category may be redundant for you.

3. Eating: Although eating food is essential to life, a two hour lunch break is not, so log the time you allocate here.

4. Sleep: We don't always understand how long we actually sleep, so log all your hours in bed resting, including midday snoozing time.

5. Other: I am not suggesting that the first four categories are the only important activities you undertake, but sticking with just five categories will make it easier to update your log regularly. For anything in this category just write a one or two word answer (such as "Facebook", "Netflix" or "date night").

Exercise Eleven   **Time prioritization: "Essential"**
For this exercise you are going to use the information that you gathered in the previous exercise to determine if you can free up any "essential" time.

Look at each of these four categories and as you analyze the time you allocated above, write down how many hours you believe you can free up in each category.

1. Work: Although you may be on a contract that doesn't allow you to reduce your work hours, a large percentage of us are work martyrs (first to arrive at work in the morning and last to leave at night). If you are doing excessive hours just because you want to feel valued, perhaps you can take back some of your own time here.

2. Travel: You might not be able to change the distance from home to work but by finding ways to optimize your travel time (such as studying via audio in the car or reading on the train) you can reclaim some of your travel time.

3. Eating: Taking the time to chew your food is better for your health than rushing your food. If you are allowed an hour or more for your lunch break, there is nothing to stop you studying whilst you are eating. Exercising after eating is not the best idea but you can train before eating to maximize lunch breaks etc.

4. Sleep: I know there are highly successful people who survive on very little sleep. I am not suggesting that you cut your sleep hours down to 4 hours a night, however, as the long term health impacts are not ideal. Unless you are sleeping ten to twelve hours a night I would suggest that rather than reducing your sleeping hours, you try to optimize them. There are lots of suggestions for better sleep, such as not drinking alcohol before bed or not looking at your smartphone/tablet screen immediately before bed. Use whatever techniques you find work best for you. By getting better sleep you are optimizing those sleep hours and this will also benefit your waking hours.

Total up all the time you have freed up in these categories.

Exercise Twelve **Time prioritization: "Other"**
Hopefully by reviewing the activities in your "Essential" categories, you've managed to optimize that time. Our next area to focus on is the "Other" category.

Because this can cover such a wide spectrum of activities (and could fill a whole book by itself) I'm just going to focus on four areas here to provide an overview and context for this category.

Look at each of these four categories (as well as any other areas that you spend time on that are not listed here) and as you analyze them, write down how many hours you believe you can free up in each of them.

- Relationships: This can cover everything from intimate relationships with a partner to social media contact with friends and family.

- Exercise: Whether you prefer sports, yoga or just getting out for the odd walk, some form of exercise is important for your health. If we were looking for a sports coach, their training would already cover this area. For anyone looking to find a coach in writing (or any other sedentary area) you must ensure that you continue to allocate some time in this area. You may not be able to play a sport as regularly whilst you are under your coach's instruction but there may be the opportunity to pick it up at a later date.

- Housework: Laundry, cleaning, cooking etc. may seem like minor activities but they can take up an inordinate amount of time. By having a set routine for these activities it can optimize the time that you spend in this area.

- Down Time: When you start trying to schedule your whole life, it can place pressure on your mental wellbeing. Without some flexibility you can easily end up burnt out or suffering from depression etc. However you choose to unwind or defrag your brain you can still set aside some time for this category. Five minutes' meditation before bed or similar activities can provide benefits and still optimize your time.

Total up all the time that you have freed up in these categories.

Exercise Thirteen   Time commitment
How much time are you willing to commit to your coach's schedule?

- From the previous exercises you should now have a total figure of how much time you have available for reallocation.
- Just because you have identified some time that you can reallocate to different activities doesn't mean that you will.
- If you really want to achieve something you will need to commit to some specific time to work with your coach. Arguably the more time you commit, the faster you will achieve your goals.

For your own health (mental and physical) I would suggest that you do not commit 100% of this time. If you are choosing to commit a high percentage of your available time to this coaching, set a specific reassessment point for this commitment. When this point occurs, you can assess your progress and possibly reprioritize some other things in your life.

Decide how much time you are committing and commit it:

- Only you can determine how much time you are willing to commit here.

- This initial amount of time may stretch you but being uncomfortable for short periods isn't necessarily a bad thing.

Confirm how much time you are allocating, write it down and commit that you have allocated this time.

50

Chapter 5   Your learning preferences

*"Formal education will make you a living; self-education will make you a fortune" – **Jim Rohn**.*

By this stage of the process, you are getting closer to determining what you are looking for in a coach, but one thing that is sometimes missed in an external search is knowing yourself (internally). Your style of learning and to some extent how you think can be critical to the speed at which you will be able to learn.

If you have done any introspection, you will probably have a general idea of your preferred way of learning. In that case I offer you this chapter more as a structured confirmation. If you have done little self-examination, or haven't thought about this subject before, this is a good place to start.

There are various psychometric testing systems out there that are predominantly designed to measure our individual mental and behavioural capabilities. These are usually employed in order to estimate our suitability for employment in a specific role.

By carrying out some testing on ourselves it can help us determine how we will best be able to utilize the resources of a writing coach.

Profile testing

There are various profile tests that rate our behavioural traits against a guide in order to determine our dominant behavioural and personality traits.

1. The Myers Briggs system divides us into sixteen possible personality types:

- ISTJ, ISFJ, INFJ, INTJ, ISTP, ISFP, INFP, INTP, ESTP, ESFP, ENFP, ENTP, ESTJ, ESFY, ENFJ and ENTJ.

2. The Disc Profiling system divides us into four possible personality types

- Dominant, Influential, Steady and Conscientious.

3. Roger Hamilton's Wealth Dynamics profiling system divides us into eight wealth profiles:

- Creator, Star, Supporter, Accumulator, Deal Maker, Trader, Lord and Mechanic.

4. Florence Littauer's Personality Plus system divides us into one of four personalities:

- Sanguine, Melancholy, Choleric and Phlegmatic.

There are many other options out there such as Tom Rath's "Strengthfinder" system or the four elements from the Tetramap model. I think you can see from this snapshot that there are many ways to classify ourselves.

Although I see these tests as guides rather than rigid limitations, I feel it is important to look at yourself before you start to look at a coach.

Finding the character and the personality of your coach
Although it isn't essential to know everything about a coach, most coaches will have done some self-examination. Once you have narrowed down your prospects to a shortlist it can be beneficial to know if your potential coach has a similar or different personality to you.

If you want to compare like for like and undergo the same test as your potential coach then it would be nice to know which tests they have done.

- A Google search under the coach's name or a search on their Wikipedia page can sometimes bring you the relevant information.
- If you can't find out the profile information on a potential coach indirectly, just contact them directly.
- By finding out which test(s) a coach has taken, you can then take the same test(s) and compare your results.

Benefitting from diversity and similarity
There are many profiling and personality systems out there and I am not suggesting that any one is better or worse than any other. You need to determine which system resonates the most with you.

Whichever system you gravitate towards, there are potential benefits from having a coach with similar or different personality to yourself.

The benefits of similar personalities
- If you think along similar lines to your coach it can make it easier to follow their system.

- If you are either both introverts or both extroverts you can see things from their perspective more easily.
- If you are a detail orientated person and so is your coach, you will approach situations from the same point of view.

The benefits of different personalities

- Choosing a coach who approaches things from a different perspective can challenge you and open you up to ideas that you wouldn't normally think of.
- As you are accountable to your coach, if you are an introvert and they are an extrovert it can help to bring you out of yourself.

Exercise Fourteen   The Personality test
Whether you are going to use your test results to compare yourself to prospective coaches or just to get to know yourself better, you can reap some benefits here.

If you are choosing a test for comparison with potential coaches, determine what information you can find out about them and choose a test that you have their results for.

- Complete the relevant personality test and compare your results with the potential coach.
- Take a note of your results and bear this in mind when you are reviewing the resources provided by potential coaches.
- If you determine that they are the same or different personality to you then review the benefits of diversity and similarity (in this chapter) during your considerations.

If you do a quick google search you will find lots of personality tests online. Although you may have your own preferences I suggest you may want to focus on one of the more popular systems such as the "DISC" or "Wealth Dynamics" system. A more popular system may make it easier to find the corresponding information on a potential coach.

N.B. Even if you decide to forgo this step of the analysis for a potential coach, a profile test can be a great start to your own journey of self-examination before you open yourself up to someone else's ideas.

Different styles of learning

If you do a google search for learning styles you will find that some have broken the number of learning styles down to three styles and some have broken them down to eight or more.

Although you may want to do some in-depth research into this at a later date, for the purpose of brevity I am only going to provide an overview of three of the traditionally recognized styles here.

The first letter of each of these learning styles has been adopted into the acronym "VAK" to make it easy to remember. Although most people use a variety of these methods to learn, there is usually one method we gravitate to as our preferred method.

Using your preferred method isn't necessarily the best way to learn a subject, but I'm a big believer in doing things that come naturally when you can.

There are several free VAK tests that can easily be found through a google search. There are also books on this subject in most good book stores (including Amazon.com).

1. V is for visual

- Visual learners tend to respond best to visual stimulus such as pictures and diagrams.
- Visual learners like to learn through written language so this is something to take into account if you determine you have a propensity to visual learning.
- It is estimated that around 65% of people veer towards learning visually.

2. A is for auditory
- Auditory learners retain information better when they hear it.
- Although there are some intimations that auditory learners often talk to themselves and read out loud, I would suggest carrying out a VAK test for a more definitive indicator.
- It is worth noting that if you are going to adopt your coach's teachings by listening to their audios that only an estimated 30% of people learn this way.

3. K is for Kinesthetic (American Spelling) or kinaesthetic (British Spelling)
- Kinesthetic learners, learn best when touching and moving.
- They like to learn by doing physical activities rather than listening to lectures.
- When you subtract the percentages from the other two styles, we can see that only 5% of the population are predominantly kinesthetic learners.

4. A simple summary of the three styles is:
- Visual: Seeing and reading
- Auditory: Listening and speaking
- Kinesthetic: Touching and doing

My own experience with the VAK test

Although I have completed several VAK tests in the past, I wanted to ensure that the information I am providing in this book is current. Whilst writing this book I completed three VAK tests myself.

Most of the tests are structured in a multiple choice style and you only get out of them what you put in. This means that the potential answers tend to be weighted on a sliding scale. Some of the first or last answers may be obviously leading you in one direction but the middle answers tend to be less obvious. If you decide to just choose the middle option predominantly (because you think the questions aren't clear enough) you will likely receive inconclusive results.

My personal opinion is that we are so used to choosing the middle option when we are reviewing something (using the likes of TripAdvisor, Amazon reviews etc.) that when we are presented with a test like this we gravitate towards the middle answer.

Be decisive with your answers!

Your results may show that you have a mixture of the three styles but if you don't get conclusive results with the first test, take another. They only tend to take ten minutes or so.

My first test

A. The first test (which had five potential answers for each of the forty six questions) gave me the following results:

- V = 34%
- A = 38%
- K = 28%

Whereas some individuals tend to score a significantly higher score in one area (and consequently a lower score in another area) I know from various profile tests I have completed that I tend to show a fairly even spread of my strengths.

Because these results were fairly evenly spread I wanted further verification, so I carried out another test from a different website.

My second test
B. This second test (consisting of thirty questions with three potential answers for each question) gave me the following results:

- V = 54%
- A= 16%
- K= 33%

Although these results seemed to indicate that I gravitate towards a visual style of learning, I determined I needed one more set of results for verification.

My third test
The third test offered me twelve statements. The first part of the statement was provided and there were then three alternative endings to the each of the statements. You had to rate the endings of each statement on a scale of 1-3 (where 3 was the most accurate description and 1 was the least).

After rating the statements you pressed "submit" and the website calculated a score for each of the learning styles.

C. My results here were:
- V = 40%

- A = 36%
- K = 24%

Although the first test results were slightly higher in the auditory learning style (something I attribute to the questions in that test being poorly framed) the final two tests showed a propensity towards the visual style of learning.

Knowing how I like to learn I believe this to be fairly accurate.

Exercise Fifteen   **The VAK Test**

Choose a VAK test and complete it.

If you do a quick google search you will find lots of free VAK tests online; just pick one and complete the test.

- If you find that you are drawn to either an online test or a book you may already be noticing a penchant for one style over another.
- Take a note of the results and bear this in mind when you are reviewing the resources provided by potential coaches.

N.B. I hope by now that you have a better idea of your own personality and learning style and that this helps you with your choice of a suitable writing coach.

Chapter 6   The main qualities you want from a coach

*"When you know what you want and you want it bad enough, you'll find a way to get it" – **Jim Rohn***

You need to be precise in what you are looking for in a coach.

The first subject I searched for a coach of my own (over two decades ago) was in the area of personal development.

I had heard of the likes of Anthony Robbins and Jim Rohn etc. but had not actively sought out anyone in this field.

One of the first personal development books I read was Robert Kiyosaki's "Rich Dad Poor Dad". It had been suggested to me by a financial advisor I met on a trip to New Zealand and I purchased it in Singapore airport on my flight back to Europe.

After reading this first book I proceeded to spend hundreds of dollars purchasing all of Robert's other books and his "Cashflow" board game. I remember spending over two hundred dollars just for the board game and then asking all of my friends to play (so that I could get my money's worth).

Although the game was great for socializing and helping reframe my outlook in some areas of finance, not all of his books were relevant to me at that time. When you aren't sure what you are searching for, you can easily get distracted and spend lots of time and money in irrelevant areas.

Today I am more selective with my choice of coach and their resources but it was only by learning from my mistakes that I reached this stage.

When we search for a coach, we are looking to improve in some shape or form. Even if you are at the top of your field, if you want to stay there continual analysis and improvement are the main ways to do so.

In order to determine exactly what you require from a coach, you need to keep asking questions and drill down to determine your end goal.

What are the main qualities you are looking for in a coach?
You may find that some of the most successful coaches span multiple areas of your writing life. You determined in the earlier chapters what you specifically want to achieve from a coach, so you need to prioritize that subject.

- They may be better known as an inspirational example of writing success rather than a coach. This could mean that in order to use them as a coach, you have to mirror their actions as presented in an autobiography, for example, rather than following a specific program.
- They may be best known as somebody who is great at publishing lots of books in a short period of time. If you are aiming for a literary masterpiece, this method of writing may not suit you.
- If they are well known for poetry or more classical writing pursuits, this can be classed as a whole different field rather than just a different genre.
- It could be that they have not coached anyone before but knowing their level of skill in their field you are willing to

approach them to coach you anyway. Perhaps they have published a large number of bestselling novels

- If they are renowned for the genre you are interested in (such as teaching nonfiction, fantasy fiction etc.) this relevance may sway your decision.
- They may have a step by step structured system for you to follow.
- They may have a high energy style of coaching that will motivate you to work through the exercises they set.
- They may have a mellow, engaging voice that will allow you to listen to their course for extended periods.

You need to determine at what level this coach is currently operating in their field. This ties in with the level of success you want them to help you achieve.

- Are you going to only use one coach from the outset or are you going to use different coaches as stepping stones towards a greater writing (or publishing) goal?
- Perhaps this coach operates at a high level but only in part of the writing process. Are they great at a specific field such as the marketing side of writing?
- If a coach has a recognized pedigree in a specific writing area but they are not operating at the ultimate level you aspire to, leveraging your previous use of this coach may help you to attract future successful coaches as you advance to the next stage in your writing career.
- Perhaps this coach is internationally renowned for their success, such as Joanna Penn, Mark Dawson, Tony Robbins, Bob Proctor or Wayne Dyer. This may mean that they have resources for all levels of progression.
- This coach may not be at the ultimate level when you first enrol with them but if (like most coaches) they are always

seeking improvement, you may be able to stay with this coach as they grow.

- In his book "The Dip", Seth Godin talks about the fact that if you are not going to be number one in your chosen business field, then you should find something else to do. This doesn't have to be your point of view but can be something to consider.

Is your potential coach ethical?

A coach being ethical should be classed as one of their main strengths, I want to emphasize this point. This may not seem obvious when you are looking for a coach but I believe being ethical is essential to coach successfully. Research into a potential coach can provide information to give you a feel whether they are known to have integrity.

There are many pre-employment work ethics and integrity tests available online. Although we can't make our new coach take an ethics test, we need to realize that we are actually employing a coach when we choose to work with them.

- This might seem subjective, but if you are going to adopt someone's system and be held to their standards, you need to be comfortable that you are going to be an apprentice to someone you admire and will be proud to emulate.
- Although you may be able to learn skills from any coach, if you have opposing values (e.g. you are a staunch environmentalist and they don't mind polluting someone's drinking water as long as they can make a few extra dollars) you are adding unnecessary stress to the relationship. Be under no illusion: you are entering into a relationship with your coach that requires commitment on both sides.

- Although you may not initially know everything about a coach, human physiology and psychology mean that the term "gut feeling" is a real thing. If you know in your gut that a person isn't ethical then it is your choice whether to proceed with this person as your coach.

- I appreciate that even the most successful coaches may have some negative information about them online, meaning your initial research may be inconclusive.

- If you find out at a later date that your coach's values clash with your own it will be your decision whether to switch coaches or not.

- If a potential coach lists false information in their resume (e.g. they say that they have written for the New York Times and they didn't) that is not a good sign.

- One issue that would raise a red flag about a coach (for myself) is if they projected opposing views in the same subject. An extreme example of this would be if a coach espouses being environmentally friendly and wanting to save the planet in public but they also invest in ravaging national parks and the environment, for mineral excavation or drilling.

During my working life I have worked for some people at a reduced rate (and at times for free) because they presented a façade of success and I believed I could learn from them.

- After working for one person for a short time it became apparent that they lacked integrity. The fact that their first reaction to most questions was a factual lie made it easy for me to identify this issue.

- As I look to take learnings from every situation, I accepted this as a great teaching moment. Knowing that adopting the methods of an unethical coach would mean compromising my own integrity I chose not to accept further employment with this individual.

- The premise of initially working for someone successful for free (or at a reduced wage) in order to learn from them is an acceptable strategy in lots of business settings. Perhaps you could consider exchanging administration work for coaching.
- Working for someone can also be a fast way of getting a true idea of their integrity.

The subject of ethics can be subjective and contentious. Before you judge someone else, determine where you are starting from.

In writing this book I undertook a couple of online pre-employment work ethics and integrity tests to determine how accurately I thought the results compared to my own perception of myself.

The first test was a 30 question integrity test:

- I received an honesty score of 78%.

The second test was a 10 question ethical test.

- I received a rating of very ethical.

I suppose most people think they are ethical; I have posted the scores here just to give you some idea of the kind of results that are possible.

Exercise Sixteen   **Determine your own ethical compass**

You can choose any of the integrity or ethical tests online (or in a book).

In this exercise I want you to complete at least one online test to see where you sit on the ethics scale.

- Find a test (through an online search, the library etc.) and complete it.
- Take these results into consideration when you are judging a potential coach.
- This is not to tell you whether you are a good or bad person.
- The purpose of taking the test is to provide you some perspective before you start judging potential coaches.

Initial Checklists

In the next chapter we are going to start the research phase of this process, so now is the time to define an initial checklist.

I suggest your checklist should have somewhere between five and ten items for your initial analysis. There is a balancing act between having enough criteria to narrow down your list of potential coaches and having too many, resulting in analysis paralysis.

Remember that this is just an initial checklist to allow you more efficient use of your time for further in-depth research.

Your initial checklist may have closer to ten points if you are looking for a writing coach in an obscure area. With over 7.5 billion people on the planet there is plenty of choice in most fields.

Some suggested checklist criteria:

- I like the sound of this coach's voice.

- They have services available within my budget of (insert your budget here).
- They have a teaching style that suits me.
- They have a structured teaching system that I can follow at my own pace.
- They can help me self-publish a business book.
- This is a structured, easy to follow course for people not comfortable with marketing.
- The potential timescale for the course is three months or less.
- The course teaches me via audio lessons or downloads.
- The course has verified reviews from authors who have increased their book sales with this coach. (You may decide to pick a minimum number of reviews here, to allow you an extra level of verification.)
- An element of the course focuses on getting book reviews.

Exercise Seventeen   Compile your checklist

In the next chapter we are going to start the research phase of this process so now is the time to define an initial checklist.

In this exercise you need to choose five to ten bullet points that represent the criteria relevant to the area of writing where you are seeking a coach.

- Use the examples above as guides or choose any other criteria that you deem relevant.
- Once you have compiled your criteria checklist, keep it handy for the next chapter.

Chapter 7   Researching and finding your coach

*"Searching represents the achievement of the goal of searching. Finding represents the achievement of the goal of finding" – **Alan Cohen***

When you have defined your criteria and you are looking for a writing coach who meets those criteria, you will be amazed at how easily you can find them.

You may have heard the idea that when you buy a red car you suddenly start to notice other red cars. These cars have always been there but you didn't notice them before because you weren't attuned to them. Now that you are attuned to search for a coach who meets your specific criteria, you will find they have been there all along, you just needed to look for them.

You may say that you know what you are looking for but you just don't know where to look. The purpose of this chapter is to provide you guidance on where to look.

The list below is not all inclusive nor do you have to use all of these resources. There are whole books available about most of these resources, so for brevity I have just provided an overview here.

I find I get my best results when I'm using a tool that I'm familiar with, so if for example you are more comfortable with using Facebook.com than using Reddit.com, I suggest you start off with Facebook.

In most cases the time spent finding your way around a new website or social media platform is not the best use of your time.

Before you start your own research, please take the time to set up some way of tracking it. Tracking is covered in more detail in the exercise section of this chapter. Once you have read through the suggestions for research below, read through the exercises next and then start your own research.

Staying focused

Once you go down the rabbit hole of online research for a coach it can be easy to get distracted.

Staying focused

In order to stay focused, I suggest you have a simple checklist of the main qualities you have determined you require in a coach.

- If you completed the exercises in the last chapter you should already have your shortlist.
- Set a minimum number of these qualities that you require in order to add a coach to your shortlist.
- (You choose between five and ten qualities in the last chapter in order to avoid analysis paralysis.)
- Simply tick off the checklist and if a coach doesn't match up, move on to the next candidate.

Building a future resource

As you search for one coach there is a good chance that you will come across prospective coaches for future needs.

- Perhaps you are searching for a creative writing coach and you come across a potential book marketing coach.
- I like to have a resources folder with documents for quotes, links to useful websites and other useful information. Taking the time to have this organized at the start of your research will save you lots of time in the future.

Search Suggestions

Remember that you don't have to use all of these options!

Google Searches

One of the first places to look is usually an internet (google) search.

Be specific in your searches:

- Typing in "Who is the greatest coach in the world" may bring up NFL or baseball coaches from years gone by, but not provide any search results relative to your writing needs.
- Typing in "Who is the world's greatest mentor" you are more likely to get results for life coaches or business mentors.

Be aware of the sponsored ads that appear when you type keywords into the google search engine. These results currently show "Ad" in the text of the information that you see. You may have to refine your search or scroll through multiple pages of search results to get relevant results.

- "Who is the best coach for writing children's picture books" or "How can I increase my Amazon book sales" are more precise questions.

No matter how great a coach is, you will usually find some negative comments about them online.

- Be aware that these comments are not always warranted and you need to make your own determinations.
- The old adage that "if someone is happy about something they will tell one person, yet if they are unhappy they will tell ten people" seems to be amplified on the internet. This doesn't mean that if there are one hundred negative comments and only twenty positive comments about a coach, you should assume this is all because of human psychology.
- It is best to use at least two or three sources of research for verification of your results.

Youtube.com and Ted.Com

When we read a book we tend to just use our own voice as we read. If you are going to spend multiple hours listening to a coach's teachings, you need to be comfortable with their teaching style (and even their voice).

If you want to know what someone sounds like, search youtube.com and see if they have videos of themselves posted there.

- Certain accents or the pitch of someone's voice may be irritating to you so watch a few of their videos and see how you feel about them.

- Perhaps they are too high or low energy. You need to determine if you will be comfortable spending multiple hours listening to this person.

Ted Talks

Ted.com hosts TED talks, which can be another good way of getting to know a coach.

- With several thousand talks on Ted.com, the site allows you to search by typing in the name of the presenter.
- Because TED talks are concise, you can look at how a coach condenses information and whether you feel they include enough relevant points for you.
- Not all coaches will have a TED talk listed and some may be old talks (which means the speaker may have improved) but this is another resource that you can use when researching coaches.

Wikipedia

The Wikipedia free online encyclopaedia provides a plethora of information about most things.

- Just typing in the name of a potential coach and "Wikipedia" can bring up a huge amount of information on them. If they don't have a Wikipedia entry it doesn't mean you should discount them as being irrelevant. This is just one of the many online resources available to you.
- Although most of the information on Wikipedia is correct and relevant, you need to be aware that Wikipedia pages can be updated by anyone, so they are not always accurate or up to date.

Reddit.com

Going down this rabbit hole can be time consuming as there are so many potential distractions on the Reddit platform.

- If you can't self-restrict your access to Facebook or Twitter, you may want to stay away from this option.
- Because Reddit is seen as "the front page of the internet" it can be a useful resource but be aware that some of the people on this platform are not always pleasant.
- You will find that the anonymity of Reddit means some users have no issue being downright mean, so be careful what you post on there.

Using it efficiently

- Search for a Subreddit in your subject. If you are looking for a specific coach you may find that there is a Subreddit solely devoted to a specific coach's resources and another giving personal opinions on the coach.
- E.g. there is one Subreddit for discussing "what you've learned from Tony Robbins" and another asking "what are your opinions on Tony Robbins and his products".
- One of the new functions Reddit allows is a profile page. If your potential coach has their own profile page on Reddit, this may be another resource for you to vet this coach.

Facebook (FB) groups

Facebook has allowed people with similar interests to connect wherever they are in the world. Ensure that you search for specific Facebook groups in your chosen writing subject.

- Type in any search term such as "kindle giveaways" "piano enthusiasts" or "indie authors" and you'll be surprised how many Facebook groups and pages that appear in your search results.

- Even though some of the groups may be classed as closed groups, that usually means you just have to ask to join (as they want to check your suitability for the group).
- If you find that a group isn't relevant to you at any stage you can always "unfollow" or "leave" that group.
- When you find a group that is useful, spend some time there and contribute. Asking questions and helping others where you can will bring you some surprising results.
- If you're like me and have lots of interests, you may need to have a review once in a while and see which of these groups are still relevant to you. I allocate time every month or two, where I prioritize all of the groups that I am currently part of, and if necessary I leave some of those groups.

Using Facebook to validate potential coaches:

- Do they have their own FB group? What quality is it and how many members does it have? Some of the top coaches will have administrators running these groups but if they are providing quality information for free, take it.
- Is your potential coach socially active in other groups? Be aware that the really famous coaches (who need staff just to run their own groups) may not have time to participate in other groups.
- Are they mentioned in other groups? If you are in a group that is relevant to your subject you will usually find that the more widely known coaches will be mentioned at some stage.
- You can ask questions in most FB groups so feel free to ask about potential coaches in these groups.

Successful friends (referrals)

You may already have successful friends who excel in the area that you are looking for a coach.

- In order to avoid uncomfortable conversations, ensure that you run them through your criteria first to ensure they are the best fit for your purpose (e.g. just having published several novels doesn't mean they are the best coach for you if you want to write nonfiction).
- Even if they aren't the ideal fit for you, let them know you are looking as they may be able to recommend someone suitable.

Your bookshelf / kindle library

You may already have used a coach's services in the past (via books etc.) so it's worth having a look at these authors and seeing if they are also suitable for the current subject.

- Remember that you are looking for the coach to meet your requirements (not just choosing someone because you like them).
- Have a quick check of any physical or eBooks that you already have and determine whether these authors make your shortlist for a coach.
- Once you start on the journey of improvement, like most successful people you will accumulate a library of resources. If you review your current resources you will likely find some relevant information to help with your current search.
- Remember to check your current library as most coaches list their other resources in the back of their books.

Amazon.com

Using the search facility in Amazon's site (in the book category) can produce more specific results than a general google search.

- As with a google search, be specific. Try typing in a term like "I want to sell more books" and the Amazon algorithm will bring you various results.
- Most coaches will have produced at least one book and this search may introduce you to coaches you haven't heard of before.
- Even world-renowned coaches who sell their products through their own websites will usually have some presence on Amazon.

LinkedIn

The LinkedIn platform used to be just a virtual business card but like most things digital it has evolved and has become more interactive.

If you don't use LinkedIn then I am not going to suggest that you must.

- I offer this as an option for research, as most of your potential coaches will have a LinkedIn profile that provides concise information about them.
- Some international coaches may have separate pages related to the relevant areas they cover, so be prepared to drill down further than just an initial search.

Subscribing to mailing lists

When researching a mentor, you may need to click on online ads and subscribe to their mailing list to get the required information. This can clog up your inbox or junk folder in the future.

There are a couple of ways to negate clogging up your primary email.

A. Unsubscribe

The first option is to unsubscribe as soon as you realize that this coach or mentor doesn't suit your criteria for this specific subject. This can have a couple of drawbacks:

- It can be hard to keep track of which sites you have unsubscribed from as you may be searching various personalities at once.
- Lots of successful coaches will have mailing lists dedicated to different subjects. You may end up on several mailing lists from the same person and although you have unsubscribed from one list, you still get emails from others.
- If at a later date you decide to vet the same person as a coach for a different subject you have to go through the whole subscribe / unsubscribe process again.

B. A vetting email address

My preferred option is to set up a separate email address just for this process:

- Choose a memorable title for the email such as "coachvetting@gmail.com". If that email address is not available you may have to add a number to make it something like coachvetting32@gmail.com but Gmail is pretty infinite so just keep trying until you find an available email address.
- When I register for this email I use a different name such as "Andrew Brown". This means that if I accidentally login to

the wrong account the name reminds me that this isn't my personal account.

- A false name also highlights that any scams addressed to this name (regarding Pay Pal accounts etc.) never need opening. You only use this name for research so you haven't got any financial info etc. in that name.
- When you register with a Gmail account google will ask you to provide a secondary email for security purposes (I use my personal email here as it makes life easier if you accidentally get locked out of this research email address).
- The benefits of using a secondary email is that you continue to receive useful information and if you are looking for a coach in a different subject you have potential coach's information all in one place.
- Once I decide to use a coach I always subscribe for their courses with either my personal or my business email. If I am subscribed to a course I don't have to wade through superfluous information sent to the email I set up for vetting to find important information.
- Remember that I don't have any financial information linked to this vetting account so if I subscribed for a course with this account, I could miss billing information and this could cause me financial issues.

Twitter, Instagram and more

You can choose to use any of the social media platforms or any other resources close at hand to search for a specific coach.

Two things that you must remember:

- Ensure that you are precise about what you are looking for.
- Don't become a victim of analysis paralysis (at some stage you need to make a choice in order to proceed).

Tracking your results

As I said at the start of this chapter, it is important to track your research. Before you start your first search, you need to have your own tracking method in place.

Whether you choose to track your research on a white board, in a spreadsheet, a notebook or any other method you prefer, it needs to be done.

My personal preference is to track with spreadsheets and below are a few suggestions of the information I log to track my progress:

A. Purpose of the coach
- I want to ensure focus so I need to know from the start why I am researching this coach.
- Am I after a creative writing coach, a marketing coach etc?

B. Search term
- Whether I am typing the term into a search engine or just formulating the question in my head, I like to know the question I am asking.
- As I am asking specific questions, I log those questions under my search terms column.
- I personally keep a separate spreadsheet of these search terms for future reference but unless you are an eternal researcher like me, you don't have to.

C. Name of the coach
- As your search starts to get results you want to start tracking who you are analysing.
- If a coaching organisation has multiple coaches, you may want to evaluate each one separately

D. Initial source

- This can be as simple as typing in "google search" or "Facebook Ad"
- If your initial source is a referral from a friend, write the friend's name.
- Just typing in where you found them can be useful for your records.

E. Links

- If you are tracking on a spreadsheet it is useful to copy and paste the link to the coach's site for future reference.
- For manual tracking you can just write the website name here.

F. Criteria Score

- This is literally the number of my criteria that this coach initially meets.
- As soon as I am able to add a score in this column, I do, as it allows me a quick initial comparison with other coaches.

G. Subscription

- To find out the required information from a coach's website, you may need to subscribe to that site.
- You tend to need a username and password for these subscriptions (although you can usually use your email as the username).
- I tend to have a column for the login username and another for the password so that I can copy and paste this info for future logins.

H. 2nd Source

I like to look for more than one source of verification and I also like to track where I've looked so that my research is carried out efficiently.

I may primarily use only a few of the search options listed in this chapter but I like to monitor where I search so that I stay up to date with new options.

I. 2nd Results
- If my second source provides little or no information to verify the suitability of a coach, I want to note this.
- I may refrain from using a source (such as Twitter or Facebook) if it isn't giving me enough information for this research.

J. 3rd Source
- As with the second source, I am just tracking where I am searching for efficiency.
- You can keep adding more columns for multiple sources but you MUST stop and choose your coach at some stage.

K. 3rd Results
- Just as with the second source, tracking whether it provides useful results will save you time later.

L. Future Use
- My research on a writing coach may identify that they are not suitable for my initial purpose (e.g. they may not help me write a novel) but they could be useful further in the writing process.
- If I see any potential usage in future I will write the area that I could use them.

- If I think they have good qualities but I am unsure how they can help, I tend to write "Maybe".
- Should there be something very negative about a coach (e.g. they have a voice that I just can't listen to for an extended period), I just write "Never".

M. Remarks

- Rather than continuing to add a never-ending number of columns to my tracker, I like a remarks column to cover any other relevant information from my search.

Exercises

Exercise Eighteen   **Set up your tracking system**
Now that you have seen how I keep track of my research, I want you to set up your own table or tracker. You can use whatever you are comfortable with but below are a few options:

- Open a blank spreadsheet on your computer or any other device and fill out your preferred column headings. Save it somewhere easily accessible to you.
- Draw a table on a whiteboard and add your column headings.
- Open a blank word document and insert a table in that document with the relevant column headings. Save it somewhere easily accessible to you.
- Open your notebook to a blank page and draw a table with the relevant column headings. Ensure that this notebook is accessible during any research period.

Now that you have your tracker set up, start to use it.

Exercise Nineteen   **The google search**

As I stated above, a google search is a great place to start your research. Remember that you must be specific in your search terms.

Type in your first search term and click on suitable links. Some examples for your search could be:

- "Who can help me write a novel"?
- "How do I get more book sales on Amazon"?
- "How do I self-publish my book"?
- "Help me write a novel".

You will get lots of results so remain focused and if you click on a link that isn't immediately relevant, go back to your search and click on a different link.

Once you have found a relevant source, rate the coach against your initial criteria (ensuring that you populate your tracker with the information).

Complete this process until you have a shortlist of three to six potential coaches.

Exercise Twenty   **Further verification**

Your initial criteria should have narrowed down your potential coaches so now we start to dig a little deeper.

Choose one website or social media platform that you are comfortable with and do a search using that coach's name.

Some suggestions for this search are

- Search for their books on Amazon.com.

- Search on relevant Facebook groups using their name (typing the name into the search box in that group).
- Search on YouTube and listen to their voice for a few minutes.
- Search Reddit forums for mentions of this coach.

Run this search for each of your shortlist of potential coaches and confirm that they still meet your initial criteria.

Exercise Twenty One   Even Further verification
If you have enough information from the previous exercise then move on and make a decision. If not, work through this exercise to provide you an extra source of research verification.

Choose a second social media platform (preferably one that you are also comfortable navigating).

Carry out a further search for these coaches to confirm they still meet your criteria.

- If your potential coaches are all scoring exactly the same, consider adding extra criteria.
- One way of tweaking your criteria is to reduce your budget.
- If your initial budget was $5000 and you reduce the limit to $4000, you can now determine which coach's services still fall within that budget.
- You may have looked for three references for a coach, try only choosing coaches with ten references. This should filter out some of the coaches.

Exercise Twenty Two   Make a decision
Although you can run your potential coaches through every search engine and social media platform available, at some stage you have to make a choice.

- If you can't reduce your shortlist down to one potential coach (all things being equal) just pick the one whose name comes first alphabetically.
- I honestly believe that by now there should be one coach that stands out as meeting your criteria.
- By choosing a coach by their alphabetical name you are not making a random choice but are avoiding procrastination, after your previous research.

In the next chapter we will look at how you are going to utilize this coach. While you are choosing how you will use a coach, if you determine your recent choice doesn't suit your needs, you can always revert back to this exercise.

If you have to revert back to this exercise, just choose the next coach in alphabetical order from your shortlist.

Chapter 8   Confirming how you will use your coach

*"Your life changes the moment you make a new, congruent and committed decision" – **Anthony Robbins***

In this chapter we are going to look at the different ways that coaches provide services and you are going to determine what kind of relationship you are going to enter into with them.

It's best to have something in writing that outlines your agreement, even if it's just a clear email that details rates, terms of service and expectations for how you'll communicate and work together. This doesn't need to be written in heavy-duty legal language, though with some coaches they will have a standard terms of service on their website.

Although we assume that technology and the internet means that everything is available at our finger tips right now, there may be some short delays in the services provided by our coaches.

Obviously the services that a coach provides will place some constraints on how you can utilize them, but lots of coaches provide multiple options and resources.

From completing the exercise in the earlier chapter of this book, you are aware which learning style suits you best.

When you take into account all of the other elements such as your budget and other commitments, you may have to choose coaching resources that are not tailored to your predominant learning style.

The three main ways that coaches coach

1. No direct contact (books and video/audio courses)

You might never meet (or have direct contact) with this coach, but by following their program, you could still achieve your goal.

Activities

- This method may entail something as simple as reading a book or watching an online video and working through the exercises included in that source.
- Although that might sound simple, it is recognized that you need to do something for at least twenty one days for it to become a habit.
- In this situation, your accountability is limited to your initial commitment that you will carry out the exercises. Although the coach produced the book (or course) they are unaware of your commitment. If you do not have strong self-discipline you may not stay on track.

In books you can determine from the outset what the exercises will be, from either the contents pages or skimming ahead through the book. A well laid out online course will also provide an overview of the exercises in the course outline. The exercises tend to be generic here and may not suit your specific needs.

Feedback

- Some online courses (such as those on thinkific.com) have automatic email reminders to track your progress through a course.
- Although most online courses will have a way of tracking your progress (usually through automated software) this still relies on you remaining self-motivated on an ongoing basis.
- Working through these exercises can mean your feedback is limited to self-satisfaction as you achieve progress towards your writing goal.

Essentially the feedback here is your own monitoring of your progress and the results if you complete the exercises.

Accessibility

- Although some audio visual resources are available for download, most of them will be hosted online and so accessibility whilst travelling can be an issue.
- There are a selection of free courses that may not be permanently available (as they tend to be marketing tools rather than quality courses) which means that you might start a course which then is not available through to achieving your writing goals.
- In contrast, if you are following the exercises in a book, you can have the book available with you all of the time.

Unless you lose access to the internet, these resources can usually be accessed on a 24/7 basis.

2. One on one coaching

One on one coaching sessions and being set tasks in between them can be one of the most efficient ways to make progress towards your goal. They can also place added pressure on the trainee (including financial pressure).

I have experienced this type of coaching on several occasions. Although it might seem that this is a more expensive option, it is a great way to be kept accountable.

If finance is an issue and you are paying for (what you perceive to be) an expensive coach, you may be more likely to undertake the tasks that the coach allocates to you.

Activities
- One on one coaching sessions tend to be scheduled at a specific time and can provide a solid structure to the coaching process.
- The coach usually sets activities or exercises for the client to carry out between sessions. Knowing that these activities will be reviewed at the next session can provide motivation and drive (as you are accountable) to achieve progress towards your goal.

Because this coaching is tailored to the client, you are not limited to set exercises. Personalized coaching can ensure much better results as long as you are prepared to be coachable.

Feedback
- During a one on one coaching session you will normally get instant feedback. This can allow you to instantly adjust the course of your journey towards your goal.
- There is traditionally an agreement for feedback between sessions (e.g. all emails will be answered within 24/48 hours)

that provides a client the confidence that they are being supported in this process.

As you progress through this process you can develop a close relationship with your coach and this means that even when you do not have direct access, you have an idea of what they expect from you. This implied feedback can allow you to proceed quickly without the need to ask unnecessary questions.

Accessibility

- With modern technology you may be accessing your coach remotely (via Skype, telephone etc.). You may even be using a coach on a different geographical continent. Scheduling your coaching sessions around a coach's available calendar, your own timetable and potential time zone differences can add to this challenge.
- For private clients there is traditionally a way of messaging directly to your coach (via email etc.) and this can alleviate some of the issues of remote coaching.

A good coach will define timeframes from the outset of the coaching process. This means that even if you may not have 24/7 access, you have the structure that allows you to progress, with the confidence that there will only be minimal times without access to your coach.

Extra interactions

One form of interaction with a coach that provides personal coaching can be working for / with them rather than in conventional coaching sessions. This may involve working for free (or for a small fee) to get first-hand experience at how to practice a skill.

- I have done this on more than one occasion and it is a great way of determining whether you and your coach have matching values.
- Because you don't know what you don't know, when you enter into an arrangement like this, ensure you have some idea of what you want out of it.
- Ensure that you have a defined timescale over which you will work for this coach (and what the recompense will be for that period). Indentured servitude is not the goal here.

This doesn't work for every situation but I include it to show you that if you have your own (thinking outside of the box) ideas, you shouldn't discount them.

3. The hybrid

This traditionally involves following a course and having some form of support during your progress.

Activities

- Although you may not have direct access to your coach, they usually have a team that they have trained in their system.
- This option tends to have most of the benefits of one on one coaching whilst being provided at a substantially lower financial commitment than direct access to a top coach.

Although the activities may not be as specifically tailored as with one on one coaching, they tend to be more flexible than a set of generic exercises in a book or automated online course.

Feedback
- A lot of modern courses provide their own communities such as closed Facebook groups. These communities usually have clients at various stages of the coaching process in them.
- You will usually find that a majority of the time when you have a question about the process, someone who started the course before you has already posted a similar question and it has been answered.
- A team tend to have specific tasks so there may be someone dedicated to chasing your progress and holding you to account.

Feedback can actually be quicker than through a one on one coaching system as you have in effect more than just one coach. Follow up in this situation may just be via regular emails. You may feel less held to account than you would if you knew that you had a regular session with a one on one coach looming.

Accessibility
- Members of the team are available to hold you to account and provide feedback / guidance where required as you are working through this course or process.
- For some of the larger coaching teams, they may have a facility for instant chat on their site.
- As all of the team members will have undergone training by a main coach, you are in effect getting access to multiple mini coaches.

This option can suit many people as it allows you some flexibility in your timetable and you can work at your own pace. If like me you like to immerse yourself in a venture, you may be able to complete modules and exercises in a shorter time frame than suggested by the coach.

Final assessments

When considering how you are going to utilize a coach there are some basic requirements that you will expect from your coach.

General services:

- Holding you to account, through tools for accountability that keep you both motivated and focused.
- Providing you clearly presented feedback and guidance to address any challenges throughout the writing process.
- Suggesting resources that can optimize the various stages of your writing journey.

A schedule or plan to progress through to your goals:

- Clear steps and exercises to ensure that you stay engaged in the programme.
- Defined milestones so that you can track your progress towards your goal (even if this is just the chapters in a book).

Exercises

If you have worked through the exercises and processes in this book you should by now have determined if a coach is suitable for you and which one best suits your needs. If you feel that you need more time to refine your decision, go back over any of the previous chapters and work through the exercises there again.

Do not use this as an excuse to procrastinate, set yourself a deadline (a maximum of a week in the future) when you will carry out the next two exercises.

Exercise Twenty Three   **Confirm what coach's services you will employ.**

You should now have determined which coaching services are best going to suit your requirements. Taking into account all of the factors that we have covered in this book (and any extra you decided to add), you now need to focus and choose what services you want to proceed with.

- Are you going to choose to be self-reliant and just use a set course or book?
- Are you going to use a coaching system that relies on the support of a team?
- Are you going to commit to employing a one on one coach?

Decide now and say out loud "I (insert your own name) have decided that to reach my goal of (insert your writing goal) I am committed to (insert your commitment here)".

e.g. "I Ged have decided that to reach my goal of writing and publishing my first novel, I am committed to enrolling on an online coaching course with Joanna Penn".

Exercise Twenty Four   **Employ your coach**

This is where the rubber meets the road. You have spent the time and effort to work through this process and I congratulate you on that. It's time to commit and connect with your resources.

From the previous exercise you have committed how you want to use a coach but perhaps you have found two coaches who provide very similar services. It's time to flip a coin.

If you truly can't choose between them then actually flip a coin and choose one as you are more than likely just procrastinating. You may be surprised that when you decide to use a coin toss to choose between two coaches, one will suddenly stand out above the other.

Do not hesitate anymore, choose your coach and then take the relevant next step:

- If you are going to follow a course from a coach's books, purchase the physical or digital versions of the books.
- If you are going to employ a one on one coach, contact the coach and notify them of your intention.
- If you are going to follow a coach's online course, get out your credit card (or Pay Pal account etc.) and enrol online now.

You should now feel good about yourself. Getting to this point in the process means you have achieved more than 90% of the population.

Over 90% of the people who sign up for a course (or buy a book like this) never complete it. Most of those people never even start!

CONGRATULATIONS, YOU ARE PART OF THE TOP 10%

You've proven you can work through the process in this book, now go work with your writing coach.

Chapter 9   Case study one - Martin

Martin is a fifty year old business coach who has been successfully coaching individuals for several years. He knows that his knowledge and experience could benefit a lot more clients if he were to condense his training systems into a book.

Although he has many skills in his chosen field, he has never written a book and he wants to produce the best possible product in an efficient manner. As a coach himself, Martin realizes the benefits of using a coach. During the early years of his career he employed coaches to enhance his own skills. Willing to be coached, he decides to look for a writing coach to help him publish this first book.

As a business owner himself he realizes the importance of having a budget and has allocated $2,000 to the employment of this coach. (That amount will include the cost of any resources supplied by this coach). Not knowing what he doesn't know, he has initially set a time budget of two months for this project. Martin understands that once he has employed a coach this timeframe may have to be modified.

1. What exactly does Martin want to achieve by utilizing a coach?

A. Phase 1   Asking the questions

What does Martin want to achieve?

- Martin wants to write a business book that encompasses his teaching systems and provide a resource for business owners.

Why does Martin want to do this?

- He wants to expand the number of clients he can service with his expertise. This would not only add a further income stream to his business but would benefit more people who could read the book.

B. Phase 2   Building the list of possibilities

How could he achieve the writing and publication of this book?

- Employ a ghost writer and just slap his name on the book.
- Muddle through writing the book himself and hope he could finish it.
- Employ a writing coach who has been successful in publishing business books.
- Employ a writing coach who is successful in helping clients produce and self-publish their own business books.
- Hire an experienced proposal writer and then pitch the book to a publishing house.
- Buy several books on "how to write a book" and work through their exercises.

C. Phase 3   Confirming the priorities of his list

Option	Priority	Remarks
Employ a ghost writer and just	4	A ghost writer will not know Martin's system as well as Martin, hence without lots of

slap his name on the book.		collaboration the finished book will be unlikely to meet his requirements. The time involved in collaboration may exceed the time it would have taken just to write the book himself. The price of a proficient ghost writer could exceed his budget.
Muddle through writing the book himself and hope he can finish it.	6	This is not really an option, as if Martin believed he was capable of this he would not have worked through this process.
Employ a writing coach who has been successful in publishing business books.	2	Just because someone has published their own book doesn't mean they are suitable to help him publish his book. The budget the coach had to publish their own book may be a lot higher than the amount that Martin has allocated for his book.
Employ a writing coach who is successful in helping clients to produce and self-publish their own business books.	1	As a coach himself, Martin knows the value of employing a coach who is geared towards a specific goal. Self-publishing will allow Martin more control of distribution and the potential for higher revenue margins.
Hire an experienced proposal writer and then pitch the book to a publishing house.	5	According to Forbes, a good proposal writer can cost from $10,000 to $15,000. Martin may not be aiming for the standard of book that will be promoted by Forbes and there is no guarantee that a publishing house would accept his proposal. He has already determined his budget and this option exceeds that amount.
Buy several books on "how to write a book" and work	3	Although this is one way of utilizing a coach, ideally he would want all of the books from one author. The fact that Martin is writing

through their exercises.		nonfiction may discount some coaches, if their books are predominantly aimed at creative writing.

D. Phase 4   Determining to focus

Having prioritized his list, what is his number one priority for achieving his goal, to write his business book?

- Martin has determined that employing a writing coach who concentrates specifically on helping people write their own successful business books is the way forward.
- This option has been prioritized as it is estimated to have the best potential for success.

E. Phase 5   Enacting his plan

Having determined his focus, Martin can now move on to the next step of the Coach Selection process.

2. Is Martin prepared to be coachable?

The fact that Martin is a coach doesn't necessarily make him a good student (just like the old adage that "Doctors make the worst patients"). He needs to be committed to being coachable and accountable.

- We were told at the start of this chapter that Martin had previously used coaches and was coachable, so that provides some reassurance that he will be coachable here.
- For the purposes of this case study I will state that Martin has agreed to be coachable.

3. What is Martin's budget for coaching services?

This is both his allocated time and finances for these services:

- Martin has allocated an initial financial budget of $2,000.
- He has allocated a two month time budget (assuming a requirement to input a maximum of ten hours a week) for this project.
- These budgets are purely for the coaching services and Martin realizes that once he starts on a program there may be other future publishing expenses such as book cover design, etc.

4. What is Martin's main learning style?

Over the years Martin has undergone many profile and strength finder tests. Of the various VAK tests he has completed, they predominantly indicate that (like 65% of the population) his primary learning style is visual.

- Written language, pictures and diagrams are some of the best potential mediums for him.
- A coach who only provides coaching via an audio course (e.g. a set of audio mp3 lessons) is not ideal as this is not Martin's primary learning style.
- These are factors that he takes into account when he is reviewing the types of resources provided by a potential coach.

5. What are the main qualities that Martin is seeking from his writing coach?

As Martin is seeking someone who has helped others succeed in writing business books he is primarily looking for:

- A proven track record of success (verifiable references from authors who they have coached).
- Someone with a teaching style that suits him.
- A structured teaching system that he can follow at his own pace.
- A coach who can help him self-publish a business book (if there is a possibility to publish through a publishing house that is just a bonus).

Martin believes that he is an ethical coach and as such is also looking for an ethical writing coach. He is not willing to compromise his own standards in this area:

- He is looking for someone who promotes a consistent message.
- He is also looking for someone who is respected in their field by a majority of people.

6.   Where did Martin find his coach?

Initial Search

Martin started off with a google search, typing in the search term "Options for writing a business coaching book".

Google Search

Quite a few of the results that showed up here were sponsored ads (they showed the "Ad" icon at the start of the website address).

By being discerning in reading the headings of the results he determined which links to click on. If a heading said "become a business coach" he knew that he could discount this result as it was not relevant to writing his book. For headings in the search results such as "book writing programs", he decided that they were worth further investigation.

By clicking on fifteen potential links he narrowed his choice down to three high probability options (the ones with the most ticks) against his checklist:

- Provides a set course designed to lead from zero to a published book.
- The cost of the course is less than $2,000.
- The potential timescale for the course is two months or less.
- The course teaches via video lessons and written downloads.
- The course has proven reviews from authors who have successfully produced quality business books.

Further verification

Having narrowed the choices down to three potential coaches he looked for further verification.

Wikipedia

- Martin typed in the names of the coaches. Although he didn't get results for all of them, the ones he found are internationally well known.
- The information available here was not the determining factor in his choice but helped him build an overall picture of the coaches' pedigrees.

Facebook Groups

- He searched on Facebook for groups under "how to grow your business by writing a book" and "how to write a business book" and joined some relevant groups.
- Asking questions in the groups about the pedigree of the three coaches brought up various responses and a mixture of respondents' experiences (some positive and some negative).
- By consolidating this information he saw that two out of the three coaches had more positive comments than negative. This was not the definitive measure to determine which coach he would use but was further verification to allow him to get an overall picture of the pedigree of these coaches.

Amazon.com

- He searched under the three coaches' names on Amazon to see what books they had available and downloaded samples of the books. You can get a good feel of someone's teaching style by the way their information is presented in their books.
- He choose two authors who had posted positive reviews on each of these coaches' websites and searched for these authors' books on Amazon.com. A reputable course should show the review and the name of the person's book who is providing positive feedback on the course. By downloading free kindle samples of these books he got a feel of the quality of the books that the course could help him to produce.

LinkedIn

- As LinkedIn is ostensibly a business networking tool, Martin used his own LinkedIn profile to search for the coaches' names and further verify their pedigrees.
- Being a business owner, Martin uses this platform regularly in his daily work and so it is a familiar resource that requires no extra training for him. If he wasn't proficient on LinkedIn, he would probably not have used this resource for this process.

7. How did Martin want to utilize his coach?

By this stage of the process Martin had found two potential coaches who compare favourably in most areas of his criteria.

As someone who is used to providing one on one coaching services, he would prefer to receive that kind of coaching himself.

- Initially he found that a limited budget of $2,000 meant that primary one on one coaching (to completion of the finished book) would not be affordable.
- His secondary choice was a coaching team that would offer a hybrid of a "one on one" coaching system.
- Quite by chance he found a course that was originally listed for $5,000 but was being promoted at a discounted price of $2,000. This was the determining factor in him choosing this coach.

Martin contacted the coach and enrolled on this coach's programme.

Chapter 10   **Case study two - Ella**

Ella is a thirty five year old mother of two children. As well as looking after her two young children she works twenty hours a week, providing administration services for the family business. Despite her hectic schedule, Ella has written and self-published three books in a fantasy series on Amazon.com. Although she has had limited success in selling her books, she believes that her books are good enough to merit purchases, if only someone knew about them.

Ella loves to write but she has always said, "I'm not a saleswoman". The whole marketing subject just confuses her. As an independent writer, she knows that she needs to do more than just write, in order for people to buy her books. She feels that she needs a structured system to help her to increase the sales of her books.

She has managed to save $1,000 which she is prepared to commit to a coach (and initial marketing). Although she has limited time available, she is committed to finding sixteen hours a week for the next three months to pursue her sales goals. Should sales take off and create sufficient revenue, she would look at replacing her part time job with more writing activities.

1.   What exactly does Ella want to achieve by utilizing a coach?

A.   Phase 1   Asking the questions.

What does Ella want to achieve?

- Ella wants to increase the sales of her current published books.

Why does Ella want to do this?

- She wants to earn some income from her current portfolio to supplement (or replace) her part time wages. Once she has learnt to market her current books, she can hopefully use the same process for her future books.

B. Phase 2   Building the list of possibilities.

How could she achieve the increased sales of her current books?

- Employ a marketing company to boost her sales.
- Buy a selection of books from Amazon.com and hope that they provide enough information for her to increase sales herself.
- Employ a writing coach who has been successful in selling their own books.
- Employ a writing coach who is successful in helping clients to sell their self-published books.

C. Phase 3   Confirming the priorities of her list.

Option	Priority	Remarks
Employ a marketing company to boost her sales.	4	The use of a specialist in marketing may initially increase her sales. Unfortunately this option will provide Ella limited potential to improve her own marketing skills for the sales of her future books.

		Her limited financial budget would also not be suitable for an expensive marketing company.
Buy a selection of books from Amazon.com and hope that they provide enough information for her to increase sales herself.	3	The financial cost of this should be within her financial budget but because she doesn't enjoy marketing, she is concerned that she will not stay focused.
Employ a writing coach who has been successful in selling their own books.	2	A writing coach who sells their own books would seem skilled in this area but Ella wants someone whose primary focus is selling Ella's books.
Employ a writing coach who is successful in helping clients to sell their self-published books.	1	This would seem the ideal option and if she can find someone within her budget, it is the one that she will pursue.

D. Phase 4   Determining to focus.

Having prioritized her list, what was her number one priority for achieving her goal to increase the sales of her books?

- Ella has determined that employing a writing coach who concentrates specifically on helping clients to sell their self-published books is the way forward.
- This option has been prioritized as it is estimated to have the best potential for success.

E. Phase 5   Enacting her plan.

Having determined her focus, Ella can now move on to the next stage of the Coach Selection process.

2. Is Ella prepared to be held coachable?

Ella is desperate for help in an area that she is uncomfortable with:

- We see in her description that Ella is looking for a structured system to provide a framework that she can follow.
- It would be a valid assumption that as she is looking for a structured system to follow she will be willing to be coached and follow a system.

3. What is Ella's budget for coaching services?

This is both her allocated time and finances for these services:

- Ella has a total financial budget of $1,000.
- She has committed a time budget of sixteen hours a week for three months to achieve her goal.
- Dependent on the success during this allocated three month period, there is the possibility for more time to be allocated after this period.

4. What is Ella's main learning style?

Ella has taken an online VAK test and determined that (like only 30% of the population) her primary learning style is audio.

- Ella prefers to learn through listening to podcasts and audio books. If Ella had opted for the option of buying a lot of books and trying to work through this process herself, she may have struggled to succeed.

- Taking these factors into account, she is looking for a coach who provides resources that she can listen to and immerse herself in the lessons.

5. What are the main qualities that Ella is seeking from her writing coach?

As she is seeking someone to help her increase her book sales, she is primarily looking for:

- A proven track record of success (verifiable references from authors whose book sales have increased).
- A structured teaching system that she can schedule around her other responsibilities.
- A person with a voice and style that she is comfortable listening to for extended periods of time.

As a mother of two children she relies a lot on her gut feeling and as such she will determine the honesty and ethics of a coach intuitively during the research process.

6. Where did Ella find her coach?

Initial Search

Google Search

Ella started off with a google search, typing in the search term "How to increase your book sales".

- Most of the results displayed were just book marketing tips.
- After clicking on a few of the links, she was a little overwhelmed and realized that she needed to refine her search to more relevant terms.

Her next search, she typed in "Coaches that increase your book sales" and got results that were a lot more relevant.

- There were lots of coaches offering various levels of services to increase book sales for authors.

By clicking on ten links she narrowed her choices down to three high probability options (the ones with the most ticks) against the following checklist:

- Provides a structured, easy to follow course for people not comfortable with marketing.
- The cost of the course is less than $1,000.
- The potential timescale for the course is three months or less.
- The course teaches via audio lessons or downloads.
- The course has proven reviews from authors who have increased their book sales with this coach.
- An element of the course focuses on getting book reviews. Ella knows that reviews are a critical factor in book sales.

Further verification

Having narrowed the choices down to three potential coaches she looked for further verification.

Amazon.com

- She searched under the three coaches' names on Amazon to see what books they had available and downloaded samples of those books. You can get a good feel of someone's teaching style by the way their information is presented in their books.
- She chose two authors who had posted positive reviews on each of these coaches' websites and searched for these authors' books on Amazon.com.
- As Ella had been monitoring her own books for quite some time she was aware of the Amazon ranking system and could estimate roughly how many books each of these authors were selling. She was interested to see whether they were selling a lot more books than she was.

Facebook Groups

- She searched on Facebook for groups under "book marketing coaches" but mainly got links for actual coaches.
- She then searched under "indie author marketing support" and found groups that were more relevant to her needs.
- Asking questions in the groups about the pedigree of the three coaches brought up various responses and a mixture of respondents' experiences (some positive and some negative).
- By consolidating this information she could see that all three of the coaches had more positive comments than negative.

7. How does Ella want to utilize her coach?

By this stage of the process, Ella has narrowed her choices down to three potential coaches who measured favourably in most areas of her criteria.

- Due to her limited budget she had discounted the idea of employing the services of a coach on a one on one basis.
- Most of the coaches provided similar hybrid structured programs, around the same price range. All of them had the potential of mp3 downloads for the course lessons.
- After further analysis she ascertained that there was little to choose between the services provided by all three of the coaches.
- Ella had previously used one of the three coach's services when she wrote her first novel.
- Already knowing the coach's style of teaching was a bonus that provided this coach an edge over the other two.
- Because she had completed a previous course with this coach, she was entitled to a discount price on this training (an Alumni discount).
- As an Alumni discount allowed Ella a free upgrade on the course that was originally within her budget, she can now afford a hybrid online course.
- This course included an initial free one on one session with the coach.

These bonuses provided Ella added confidence and she chose to enrol on this course.

N.B. It is worth noting that although Ella chose a coach she had previously used, this was only after suitable analysis and comparison with other potential coaches. There is nothing wrong with using a coach you have used previously, as long as you have confirmed their suitability for your needs.

Chapter 11   **Case study three - David**

David is a twenty six year old male. He has written and published ten nonfiction books on Amazon.com and they are bringing in sufficient cash flow that he can focus on writing full time.

Although he may seem relatively young, he excels in absorbing information and is constantly looking at ways to be more efficient through self-examination. From an early age he was a creative child and has always enjoyed drawing and writing short stories.

David is very interested in branching out into fiction writing. He is fully aware that there is a difference between writing structured "how-to books" and writing fictional narratives with compelling characters.

Whilst researching for his previous nonfiction books he has seen plenty of books for sale with titles such as "How to write a novel in 30 Days". He is not convinced that with his current skillset he could produce a book of sufficient quality in such a short time frame. Not being someone to do anything by half measures, he is only interested in writing quality products.

He knows that his first novel may not be perfect but he has tentatively allocated a budget of $5,000 in cash and a six month time period to complete this project.

1. What exactly does David want to achieve by utilizing a coach?

A. Phase 1   Asking the questions

What does David want to achieve?

- David wants to write and publish his first novel.

Why does David want to do this?

- He wants to expand his writing portfolio and branch out into the realm of fiction writing.

B. Phase 2   Building the list of possibilities

How could he achieve the writing and publication of this book?

- Buy a selection of books from Amazon.com on creative writing and use his current skillset to publish a novel.
- Sign up for a creative writing course and use his current skillset to publish a novel.
- Employ a writing coach who teaches and mentors first time fiction writers to write a novel, including the whole process through to publishing.
- Employ a writing coach who teaches how to write a novel and use his current skillset to publish a novel.

C. Phase 3   Confirming the priorities of his list

Option	Priority	Remarks
Buy a selection of books from Amazon.com on creative writing and use his current skillset	4	Being a nonfiction writer he realizes the benefits of "how-to books" but he also knows that he learns best by partnering with

to publish a novel.		someone who has excelled in their field.
Sign up for a creative writing course and use his current skillset to publish a novel.	3	He has worked through several creative writing exercises in the past but believes that as he is working to quite a tight deadline, he needs more focused help.
Employ a writing coach who teaches and mentors first time fiction writers to write a novel, through to publishing.	1	David perceives this to provide the best opportunity for success within his set time frame. Once he has learned this process he believes that he may not need as much hands on coaching for any future fiction publishing.
Employ a writing coach who teaches how to write a novel and use his current skillset to publish a novel.	2	Although this would provide the benefits of a coach (at a potentially lower financial cost) as this is his first novel, he wants to master the idiosyncrasies of fiction publishing first.

D. Phase 4   Determining to focus

Having prioritized his list, what is his number one priority for achieving his goal of writing his first novel?

- David has determined that he needs to employ a writing coach who will teach him how to write his first novel, through to publishing.

E. Phase 5   Enacting his plan

Having determined his focus, David can now move on to the next stage of the Coach Selection process.

2. Is David prepared to be held coachable?

We are told that David has undergone a lot of self-examination and is always looking for ways to be more efficient.

- It is not a stretch to assume that someone like this would be willing to be accountable to a coach (if this is the optimum way of progressing in this writing project).

3. What is David's budget for coaching services?

This is both his allocated time and finances for these services:

- David has allocated an initial financial budget of $5,000.
- He has allocated a six month time budget (assuming a requirement to input a maximum of thirty hours a week) for this project.

4. What is David's main learning style?

David has taken many personal development tests in the past and knows that he learns best through audio visual input.

- David is an avid learner and prefers to learn via video type mediums.
- He absorbs information easily so is happy for continual feedback and the ability to learn at an accelerated pace.

5. What are the main qualities David is seeking from his writing coach?

As David is seeking someone who could help him succeed in writing a novel he is primarily looking for:

- A proven track record of success (verifiable references from authors who they have coached).
- Someone with a teaching style that suits him.
- A structured teaching system that he can follow at his own pace.
- He is looking for someone who promotes a consistent message.
- He is looking for someone who is respected in their field by a majority of people.
- Someone providing services within the constraints of his financial budget.
- Someone with a high energy teaching style.
- Someone who has published their own novels successfully (leading by example).

6. Where did David find his coach?

Initial Search

David has his own Facebook group with over twenty thousand followers so he decided to utilize this valuable resource to do most of the research for him.

Facebook Groups

He set up a competition on his FB page

- The competition asked subscribers of his page to email him their feedback of coaches they had used (these results were sent to an email address set up just for this competition).
- He provided a specific template of the information that he wanted from the feedback. This included prices of the coach's fees etc.
- Feedback was to be in the form of a table with the ten criteria rated one or zero for compatibility and the total score out of ten (along with the coach's name) noted in the title of the email.
- He offered a boxed set of his current books as a prize to the top ten testimonials.
- The competition received over five hundred entries and David decided that having an assistant consolidate this information was the best option.

N.B. This competition was also planting the seeds for future promotion of his completed novel.

Further verification

David had the assistant collate the reviews and determine the top six coaches (with the highest aggregated scores).

Facebook Groups

He then ran a survey on his FB page.

- The survey asked the subscribers to the page to choose one of the six coaches as their preferred option, for a coach to help someone write a novel through to publication.
- He chose the three coaches with the most votes for further consideration.

Online research

Up until now the heavy lifting of the research had been done by others but as he would be the one working with this coach he took over the final verification with his own online research.

- He initially searched for these three coaches on YouTube to determine how he felt with their voices and cadence.
- Narrowing the choices down to two of the three options, he next looked at their websites and confirmed what services they actually provided.
- He searched on Amazon and downloaded samples of two novels from each of the coaches.

As he was in effect just verifying the research of the subscribers to his Facebook page, this was more to get a gut feel of the coach that he felt he would be most comfortable with.

7. How does David want to utilize his coach?

David now had two potential coaches that measure favourably in most areas of his criteria.

He had chosen two coaches that he liked to listen to (from his YouTube research) and ideally wanted a one on one coaching relationship.

- He contacted both of the coaches directly, explaining his current progress in nonfiction publishing and asking how they would be able to service his needs.
- The feedback from both was positive and the price ranges were both reasonably similar.

- During his conversation with one of the coaches, they indicated an interest in publishing some of their own nonfiction books.
- As neither of the coaches' one on one services would be within his $5,000 budget, David brokered a deal where he would exchange some of his own expertise for publishing nonfiction with one of the coaches of fiction.
- This exchange was the deciding factor with David's choice and brought the coach's services within his set budget.
- David would have a session scheduled every two weeks with his coach and part of these calls involved an exchange of information in both directions.
- David perceived that with the dedicated one on one coaching he would achieve his goal of publishing his first novel within the six month timeline.

David contacted the coach and enrolled with this coach's programme.

Chapter 12   Case study four- Giselle

Giselle is a sixty year old retired school teacher. She has a cache of writing but has never published anything commercially.

Technically she is retired but practically she still has a keen mind and wants to earn a little extra cash to supplement her pension. Many people have told her that with schemes such as KDP (Kindle Direct Publishing) on Amazon.com there is no need for a traditional publisher. It has been suggested by friends and relatives that the process of self-publishing can be relatively cheap and she should investigate this further.

Although she has lots of poetry, some short stories and various other literary works (that she has written over the years) she has never released the novel that she believes is inside of her.

As a former teacher, Giselle Knows that age is no barrier to learning and believes she can expedite the process if she employs the right coach.

As a retiree she can allocate a reasonable amount of time to this project but is hoping that she can complete her first novel within six months.

With a set income she has allocated $500 of her savings to pay for a coach's resources.

1. What exactly does Giselle want to achieve by utilizing a coach?

A.   Phase 1   Asking the questions

What does Giselle want to achieve?

- Giselle wants to publish her first novel and progress to future literary publication of some of her current portfolio.

Why does Giselle want to do this?

- She wants to continue to keep her mind active but primarily to start to financially supplement her pension.

B.   Phase 2   Building the list of possibilities

How could she achieve the writing and publication of this first novel?

- Buy a selection of books on creative writing and Amazon marketing, hoping that this brings her success.
- Sign up for some creative writing courses to hone her skills and then buy a selection of books on Amazon book publishing and marketing, hoping that this brings her success.
- Employ a writing coach who teaches and mentors first time fiction writers through to novel publication.
- Sign up for some creative writing courses to hone her skills and then employ a writing coach who teaches how to publish a novel.

C.   Phase 3   Confirming the priorities of her list

Option	Priority	Remarks
Buy a selection of books on creative writing and Amazon marketing, hoping that this brings her success.	4	Although she has quite a bit of creative writing experience, she has never progressed to having a novel published. She would prefer a system that hones her writing skills and covers the whole publishing process.
Sign up for some creative writing courses to hone her skills and then buy a selection of books on Amazon book publishing and marketing, hoping that this brings her success.	3	Even with Giselle's history of creative writing she realizes the benefits of honing her skills for publishing. As with the option above she would prefer a system with more guidance.
Employ a writing coach who teaches and mentors first time fiction writers through to novel publication.	1	This is her preferred choice as it encompasses all of her needs in one place.
Sign up for some creative writing courses to hone her skills and then employ a writing coach who teaches how to publish a novel.	2	Although the writing courses may mean that she is more prepared when she employs her coach, this could extend the time to completion of her novel. The cost of the extra courses could also impact on her budget for a coach.

D.   Phase 4   Determining to focus

Having prioritized her list what is her number one priority for achieving her goal to write her first novel?

- Giselle has determined that the best way for her to achieve her writing goals is to employ the resources of a writing coach who teaches and mentors first time fiction writers through to publication.

E.   Phase 5   Enacting her plan

Having determined her focus, Giselle can now move on to the next stage of the Coach Selection process.

2. Is Giselle prepared to be held coachable?
- As a long time teacher Giselle understands the benefits of listening to a coach or teacher.
- She has built her career on coaching others and is determined to be accountable to her coach to gain the best results.

3. What is Giselle's budget for coaching services?

This is both her allocated time and finances for these services:

- Giselle has allocated an initial financial budget of only $500.
- She has allocated a six month time budget and is prepared to commit forty to fifty hours per week (should the training require) to achieve success in this project.

4. What is Giselle's main learning style

- Having attended numerous (too many to mention) training courses and lectures over the years, Giselle knows that she learns best from audio visual input.

5. What are the main qualities Giselle is seeking from her writing coach?

As Giselle is seeking someone who can help her succeed in publishing her first novel she is primarily looking for:

- A proven track record of success (verifiable references from at least four authors whose book sales they have coached to increase).
- A structured, easy to follow course for people not comfortable with publishing.
- The cost of the course is less than $1,000.
- The potential timescale for the course is six months or less.
- The course teaches via video / audio lessons or downloads.
- An element of the course focuses on honing her creative writing skills. Giselle knows that just because she has written lots, doesn't mean that she has written well.

6. Where did Giselle find her coach?

Initial Search

Google Search

Giselle started off with a google search, typing in search terms:

Initially she typed in "How to write and publish a novel."

- Most of the results displayed were more writing and marketing tips than a coach's services.
- After clicking on a few of the links, she was a little overwhelmed and realized that she needed to refine her search more.

Her next search, she typed in "writing and publishing my first novel" and got results that were slightly more relevant.

- There were some coach's services available but again the information was not all relevant.

Her final search she typed in "fiction writing coaches" and got results more relevant to her needs.

- By getting focused on exactly what she wanted, her search provided much more suitable results.

By clicking on ten links she narrowed her choice down to three high probability options (the ones with the most ticks) against her previous checklist:

- Provides a structured, easy to follow course for people not comfortable with publishing.
- The cost of the course is less than $1,000.
- The potential timescale for the course is six months or less.
- The course teaches via video / audio lessons or downloads.
- The course has proven reviews from (at least four) authors who have increased their book sales with this coach.
- An element of the course focuses on honing her creative writing skills. Giselle knows that just because she has written lots, doesn't mean that she has written well.

Further verification

Amazon.com

Now that Giselle has narrowed down her choices for writing coaches she is ready for the next stage of her research:

- She searched under the three coaches' names on Amazon to see what books they have available and downloaded samples of the books. You can get a good feel of someone's teaching style by the way their information is presented in their books.
- She chose two authors who had posted positive reviews on each of these coaches' websites and searched for these authors' books on Amazon.com.
- As Giselle isn't fully aware of what is classed as a good book she uses the number of reviews as her measure. Having bought lots of products from Amazon.com in the past she is comfortable with the review system. Rather than set a benchmark of a (specific) number of reviews, she just took a record of the number of reviews that each book had posted.
- Comparing the number of reviews for each coach and their authors gives her an idea of the success of these coaches.

Facebook Groups

For the final stage of her verification, Giselle decided to look at Facebook groups. This choice was swayed partly by the fact that Facebook is another online tool she is familiar with.

- She searched on Facebook for groups under "self-Publishing".
- This resulted in multiple groups and pages.
- She then joined several of these groups.

- Asking questions in the groups about the pedigree of the three coaches brought up various responses and a mixture of respondents' experiences (some positive and some negative).
- By consolidating this information she could see that two of the three of the coaches have more positive comments than negative.

7. How does Giselle want to utilize her coach?

Because of her limited financial budget she is looking to utilize coaching resources that favour the fact that she has lots of time available (rather than cash). This discounts the option of one on one coaching.

By this stage of the process Giselle had narrowed her choices down to two potential coaches who measured favourably in most areas of her criteria.

- Due to her limited budget she had discounted the chances of employing the services of a coach on a one on one basis.
- She found one coach who offers an online course on writing and publishing your first novel for only $300.
- This course has a set structure of lessons and a weekly newsletter (which has FAQs from course members).
- The price of the course and the 30 day money back guarantee mean that she had limited risk with a high potential upside.

Taking all of these factors into consideration she enrols for the online course.

Appendix A   Coach selection checklist

The purpose of this checklist is to provide you a consolidated list to track your progress through the Coach Selection process.

Ser	Step	Actions	Remark	check
1	Determining what you want from a coach.	Complete the 5 Phase process A-E.		
2	Committing to accountability.	Confirm your commitment.	If you can't commit, then quit now!	
3	Setting your budget.	How much time and money will you commit to the project?		
4	Deciding on your learning preferences.	Confirm your preferences.		
5	Determining the main qualities you want from a coach.	Compile your checklist.		

6	Searching and choosing your coach.	Research potential coaches.		
7	Determining how you will use the coach.	Confirm how you will utilize this coach's resources.		
8	Taking Action.	Complete the enrolment and agree to the contract with the coach.		

Appendix B   Glossary

2

- **24/7**   A term in commerce and industry that means a service is available anytime. Twenty four hours a day, seven days a week.

A

- **Algorithm**   A set of steps in mathematics (and computer science) that are performed to provide the results of a calculation or automated reasoning task. The steps are performed in a set process and in relation to computers are followed automatically. Most search engines (online or otherwise) function by the use of an algorithm. By searching for keywords and phrases, the algorithm in a search engine attempts to provide results that best match the words typed in to the search field.

- **Alumni (singular Alumnus)**   Alumni refers to a former members of an association or former students of a college, course or school.

- **Alumni Discount**   A discount afforded to former students.

- **Amazon (an abbreviation of Amazon.com,)**
  The largest online retailer in the United States and the parent company of various other Amazon online retailers such as Amazon.co.uk in the UK. Although there will be very few people who have not heard of this company, I just wanted to reiterate that the terms are interchangeable in this book.

- **Analysis Paralysis**   This term refers to the situation where an individual spends so much time analysing a situation that they end up not making any progress. A lack of decision in this circumstance means that you can spend so much time analysing your options that you never make a choice.

B

- **Blog (abbreviated from weblog)**   A regularly updated website or web page written in a more informal, conversational style than more traditional websites.

- **Blogger**   A person who updates a blog (frequently).

- **Buyer's Remorse**   A sense of regret after having made a purchase. Frequently associated with an expensive purchase.

C

- **Cadence** Cadence can be classed as a harmonic configuration at the end of a phrase but in relation to someone's speech it can mean their general way of speaking.

- **Case Study** This term traditionally refers to an in depth study of a particular situation rather than a sweeping statistical survey. For the purpose of this book the term refers to a worked example of the process, to provide guidance and further clarification of the system.

- **Cashflow Game** A board game developed by Robert Kiyosaki as a fun way of delivering financial education.

D

- **Date Night** A prearranged occasion on which an established couple go for a night out together. Traditionally a way of busy couples ensuring they make time for each other.

- **Defrag your brain** Defrag is a shortened version of the word defragment. Usually used to describe the process of tidying up computer memory. When referring to defragment of the brain we traditionally mean to allow it to return to its natural state of order (after a period of hectic thinking).

F

- **Facebook.Com (Facebook)** A social networking website that makes it easy for you to connect and share with your family and friends online.

- **Facebook Group** A place on the Facebook.com platform that allows individuals to share their common interests and express opinions.

- **Frequently Asked Questions (FAQ)** A set of questions and answers that are the most frequently asked in a certain context.

G

- **Google Searches** A recognised term for an internet search. Because the google company is so dominant in the online search field, the term google has been adopted as a verb. To google and to search online are now interchangeable in the English language.

- **Gut feeling** A feeling of intuition, whereby we know things without consciously reasoning.

H

- **"How-to" books**   Nonfiction books that are written with the purpose of providing the reader the information on how to complete a task. An example of this would be a book on "How to play Golf", written to help the reader complete the task of improving their golf game.

- **Hyperlink (Link)**   A word, image or phrase that allows you to jump to a new document or a new section within the current document. The redirect can be activated by clicking, tapping or hovering over it.

- **Indentured servitude**   This term traditionally referred to a person under contract to work for another person for a defined period of time, usually without pay, in exchange for passage to a new country. Although there are some differences between indentured servitude and slavery, both classes of people were considered property before the American Civil war.

- **Independent (Indie) Author**   An independent author is an author who is the creative director of their own books from concept to completion and beyond. There is no separate publisher involved.

- **Instagram**   A social networking app made for sharing photos and videos from a smartphone.

K

- **Keywords**   Keywords refers to specific words or phrases that an algorithm (in a search engine) deems relevant, during a search.

- **Kindle Direct Publishing (KDP)**   A program provided by the Amazon Company that allows authors and publishers to publish their books worldwide to be read on kindles or kindle apps.

L

- **LinkedIn**   A social networking site designed specifically for the business community.

M

- **Mailing lists**   A list of names and addresses (or email addresses) of people to whom advertising matter, information, or material is sent.

- **Mentor**   A mentor is traditionally defined as a professional relationship (although most mentors affect lifestyles and not just work) where an experienced individual provides knowledge, support and encouragement to help an individual meet their potential.

N

- **N.B. (Nota Bene)** Nota Bene is a Latin term that translates into English as "note well". The term is abbreviated to N.B. and when it precedes a statement or a sentence it is there to emphasize an important point in a body of writing.

- **Netflix** A streaming service that allows subscribers to stream movies, TV shows or other video formats to their TV or digital device through the internet.

O

- **Opportunity Costs** This relates to the potential costs (in time or money) that you are incurring by investing in a specific endeavour. If you invested $100 in a lottery ticket and didn't win the cost would be your $100 stake plus any potential revenue that you could have made from investing that money elsewhere.

P

- **Pen name** A pen name is a fictitious name that an author writes under that is not the same as the name they use in their everyday life. Authors tend to use different pen names if they write in different genres in order to differentiate their works in these genres (or to disguise their true identity when writing in a contentious area). A pen name can also be shared by different authors in order to provide perceived continuity of authorship.

R

- **Reddit (Reddit.com)** Reddit is an entertainment, social news networking service and news website. Also known as the front page of the internet, this website allows individuals to interact and comment on anything in the universe.

- **Return On Investment (ROI)** A ratio calculating how much money was made on an investment as a percentage of the purchase price.

- **Reviews** In modern society it has become a recognized norm that we are expected to provide ratings for any business services that we receive. Whether we are rating our experience with Uber drivers or accommodation reviews (on the likes of TripAdvisor) we are becoming conditioned to do this. When we refer to reviews with regards to writing we are predominantly focused on the book reviews and ratings that are placed on book sites (such as Goodreads or Amazon.com). If we are looking for a coach to help us market books, we may want guidance on receiving reviews. These reviews can make a big difference in the quantities of our book sales.

- **Reviews (also short for customer reviews)**
written feedback placed against your Amazon book listing (either positive or negative) that contributes to the ranking of your product listing.

- **Robert Kiyosaki**   An internationally renowned writer and business investor, best known for his "Rich Dad Poor Dad" book series.

S

- **Self-Made Man/Woman**   A person who was born poor or otherwise disadvantaged, but who achieves economic or other success thanks to their own hard work and ingenuity rather than family connections or other privileges. That may be the technical term but some individuals use the term "self-made" to indicate that they didn't need any assistance in getting where they are.

- **Self-Publishing**   In relation to books this refers to the publication of a book by its author without the involvement of an established publisher.

- **Skin in the game**   The term "skin in the game" refers to the situation where someone is at risk financially because they are invested in something that they want to happen. If you paid for 1,000 of your own books to be published, the cost of the publishing would be at risk against any potential sales (in this situation you would have skin in the game).

- **Social media**   This term refers to computer mediated technologies that facilitate the creation of information via virtual networks and communities. Twitter and Facebook are just two examples of the many platforms that allow this sharing.

- **Subreddit**   A forum dedicated to a specific topic on Reddit.com.

T

- **TED Talks**   Influential videos from expert speakers on a multitude of subjects, ranging from education to business, science and more. Hosted on TED.com.

- **Terms Of Service**   The Terms of service are the rules and regulations that you must adhere to in order to partake of the services of an individual or organisation. Well known Terms of Service are the agreements that customers agree to in order to use a smart phone on a mobile network.

- **The Richest Man in Babylon**   A classic 1926 book that dispenses financial advice through a collection of parables set in ancient Babylon.

- **Think and Grow Rich** A classic 1937 book renowned as a self-help and personal development book.

- **Thinking outside of the box** A metaphor that refers to thinking unconventionally or from a new perspective. Customarily a way of solving problems when conventional solutions don't provide the required results.

- **Twitter (twitter.com)** An online social networking service that enables users to send and receive messages no longer than 140 characters long.

V

- **VAK System (Visual, Auditory, and Kinesthetic)** A system of learning that identifies individuals' predominant method of learning.

W

- **Wikipedia** Wikipedia is a free online encyclopaedia that can provide a plethora of information about most things. As it can be updated by anyone that wants to take the time to add information to a listing, the information may not always be 100 % accurate.

- **Work Martyrs**   An employee who works themselves to the bone because they believe they're the only ones who can do their job.

Y

- **YouTube (Youtube.com)**   A video sharing platform where you can deliver video you have created or view a video others have created. This platform has videos of everything from kittens playing a piano to instructions for you to build a cabin out of logs.

Appendix C   Consolidated exercises

Exercise One   **What are you trying to achieve**
Determine what you are trying to achieve and write this in a one sentence statement e.g.

- I want to supplement my business coaching services by writing a book in my field.
- I want to publish my first novel.
- I want to build a long term career as an author.

Exercise Two   **Determine your Why**
Determine why you want to achieve this and write this in a one sentence statement e.g.

- I want to be in charge of my own financial destiny.
- I want to tell the story of my family before I die.

Exercise Three   **Compile your list**
Write a list of options to achieve this goal (up to ten but a minimum of three) to allow you to focus on the solutions for your goal.

However you have compiled your list (spreadsheet, word document etc.), a table is one of the best options. You only need two columns for this table.

- List all of your options in the left hand column of the table
- Write freely and don't worry how "outside of the box" these ideas seem.
- The main thing here is to just compile your list.

Exercise Four   Prioritize your list

Once you have completed the last exercise you should now have a table with the left hand column full of options to achieve your goal and the right hand column empty.

Now to prioritize:

- In the right hand column allocate a number against each option based on how likely this option is to help you achieve your goal.

- Allocating the number "one" for the option with the highest probability for success, then number "two" for the next highest probability, and so on and so on.

Exercise Five　　　　　**Historical accountability**

Most of us have been accountable in some shape or form in our past but we can't always recount those situations.

In this exercise, I want you to list any time in the past when you have either been accountable to someone else or held yourself accountable. This doesn't have to be anything major, I just want you to remember that you have previously been accountable for something.

Below are a few general suggestions:

- Studying for exams - This can relate to any level of education as there are always potential distractions.
- Completing your school homework – As children there are ways and means to avoid homework but if you completed it regularly, you held yourself accountable.
- Saving money to purchase something - This could be something that you saved for as a child or perhaps a deposit for a car or house (later in life).
- Adhering to a curfew that you had to be home by as a child.
- Completing exercises in your own time (with no supervision) as set by a sports coach.
- Practicing a musical instrument or dance routine for a performance.

The bullet points that I have included above are just a few general examples and most people can probably relate to at least one of them. Feel free to use any of these examples or recount an instance more relevant to your own circumstances.

Exercise Six   **Rating your success**

Once you have recounted several times when you have been accountable, I want you to rate those instances of accountability.

- Rate the success of your results on a scale of zero to five (with zero being total failure and five Being total success).
- If you rate any results at a three or above then those situations can be classed as being successful in holding yourself to account.
- If you rate any results at a two or below then those situations can be classed as being unsuccessful in holding yourself to account.
- Try to remember at least one time where your accountability provided a successful outcome and another where it did not.

If you can't remember anytime that your accountability resulted in a successful outcome, it doesn't mean that you aren't coachable. You may just need to be extra steadfast when making your new commitments.

If you can't remember anytime that your accountability resulted in a failed outcome that doesn't mean that you don't need a coach. You just might have an advantage in maintaining the coaching agreement.

Exercise Seven   **Checking your current accountability**

The previous two exercises where designed to help you focus on an accountability frame of mind. Whatever your previous results, it doesn't guarantee whether your future accountability attempts will be successful or not.

In order to refresh your mental state and prove that you can hold yourself to account, I want you to undertake the following exercise:

- For the next seven days I want you to record the statement "I (insert your name) am willing to be coachable).
- You can choose to use a voice recorder, write in a notebook or make a note on your smartphone.
- You choose a specific time that is suitable to you (if you need to set an alarm on your phone or in your calendar).
- I want you to record this at the same time for seven days because this time period will span a weekend. Most people who plan their weekdays around work don't hold themselves to the same standards at weekends.

Exercise Eight   Financial Spending

In this exercise I want you to determine how much money discretionary spending that you have available to commit to a writing coach.

As most of us make our payments digitally nowadays, it can be relatively easy to look back over our bank and credit card statements to track our spending.

You need to list where you allocate all of your income. Use the four categories below to help you list your expenditure:

A. Household Expenses
- List all of your monthly expenses (utilities, fuel etc.).

B. Business Expenses
- This may be easy to calculate, if you don't currently run a business it should be zero.

C. Savings
- You may have automated savings coming out of your income.
- As compound interest works best when you start to save early, I am not recommending that you stop contributing to your savings.

D. Discretionary Spending
- This includes any social spending but also any expenses that can be reduced.
- If you have a mobile phone plan or a cable TV package can you reduce these costs?
- If you have credit card payments can you negotiate to get the payments reduced?

N.B. The sum total of all of these figures should total your income. If not go back and check your figures.

Exercise Nine   **Financial Commitments**

Now that you have determined where you spend your money, you need to determine how much of your discretionary spending you are willing to commit to your writing coach.

Just because you have an amount of funds available, does not mean that you should commit it all. Although you may be able to estimate the financial benefits of using this coach there are no 100% certainty's in your R.O.I.

Before you commit any finances you need to decide what the total loss of this money with no financial benefits would mean to you.

Paying for a coach with your credit card with the hope that the financial returns that a coach provides will pay off this credit card is not advisable.

If you discovered in the last exercise that you haven't got any discretionary funds available, you may need to create some extra income.

Decide how much you are committing financially and commit it.

- Only you can determine what amount of money you are willing to risk here.
- Confirm your amount, write it down and commit that you are allocating these funds.

Exercise Ten   **Time monitoring**
For this Exercise divide the next seven days into 15 minutes segments and log where you spend that time.

You can choose to track this in a spreadsheet or in a notebook but I encourage you to update this log as often as possible. There are productivity apps (such as "Focus Keeper) that allow you to set a timer for a 15 minute period, feel free to use one of these if it helps you.

If you choose to list your activities at the end of each day (rather than regularly updating your log during the day) you may find it hard to remember how much time you devoted to each activity.

Rather than trying to classify your time into lots of categories I find that just using the following five categories works best for me:

1. Work: This relates to any income generating activity.

2. Travel: This relates to travel to and from work so if you work from home this category may be redundant for you.

3. Eating: Although eating food is essential to life a two hour lunch break is not necessarily the same thing so log the time you allocate here.

4. Sleep: We don't always understand how long we actually sleep so logging your hours in bed resting (or a midday snooze can all be logged here).

5. Other: I am not suggesting that the first four categories are the only important activities you undertake, but sticking with just five categories will make it easier to update your log regularly. For anything in this category just write a one or two word answer (such as Facebook, Netflix or date night).

Exercise Eleven   **Time prioritization "Essential"**
For this exercise you are going to use the information that you gathered in the previous exercise to determine if you can free up any "essential" time.

Look at each of these four categories and as you analyze the time that you allocated above, write down how many hours you believe that you can free up in each category.

1. Work: Although you may be on a contract that doesn't allow you to reduce your work hours a large percentage of us are work martyrs (first to arrive at work in the morning and last to leave at night). If you are doing excessive hours just because you want to feel valued, perhaps you can take back some of your own time here.

2. Travel: You might not be able to change the distance from home to work but by finding ways to optimize your travel time (such as studying via audio in the car or reading on the train) you can reclaim some of your Travel time.

3. Eating: Taking the time to chew your food is better for your health than rushing your food. If you are allowed an hour or more for your lunch break, there is nothing to stop you studying whilst you are eating. Exercising after eating is not the best idea but you can train before eating to maximize lunch breaks etc.

4. Sleep: I know there are highly successful people who survive on very little sleep but (as the long term health impacts are not ideal) I am not suggesting that you cut your sleep hours down to 4 hours a night etc. Unless you are sleeping ten to twelve hours a night I would suggest that rather than reducing your sleeping hours you try to optimize them. There are lots of suggestions for better sleep, such as not drinking alcohol before bed or not looking at your smartphone/tablet screen immediately before bed. Use whatever techniques you find work best for you, by getting better sleep you are optimizing those sleep hours and this will also benefit your waking hours.

Total up all the time that you have freed up in these categories.

Exercise Twelve   Time prioritization "Other"
Hopefully by reviewing the activities in your "Essential" categories, you've managed to optimize that time. Our next area to focus on is the "Other" category.

Because this can cover such a wide spectrum of activities (and could fill a whole book by itself) I'm just going to look focus on four areas here to provide an overview and context for this category.

Look at each of these four categories (as well as any other areas that you spend time and are not listed here) and as you analyze them, write down how many hours you believe that you can free up in each of them.

1. Relationships: This can cover everything from Intimate relationships with a partner to social media contact with friends and family.

2. Exercise: Whether you prefer Sports, Yoga or just getting out for the odd walk, some form of exercise is important for your health. If we were looking for a sports coach their training would already cover this area. For anyone looking to find a coach in writing (or any other sedentary area), you must ensure that you continue to allocate some time in this area. You may not be able to play a sport as regularly whilst you are under your coach's instruction but there may be the opportunity to pick it up at a later date.

3. Housework: Laundry, cleaning, cooking etc. may seem like minor activities but they can take up an inordinate amount of time. By having a set routine for these activities it can optimize the time that you spend in this area.

4. Down Time: When you start trying to schedule your whole life, it can place pressure on your mental wellbeing. Without some flexibility you can easily end up burnt out or

suffering from depression etc. However you choose to unwind or defrag your brain you can still set aside some time for this category. Five minutes meditation before bed or similar activities can provide benefits and still optimize your time.

Total up all the time that you have freed up in these categories.

Exercise Thirteen   Time commitment

How much time are you willing to commit to your coach's schedule?

- From the previous exercises you should now have a total figure of how much time you have available for reallocation.
- Just because you have identified some time that you can reallocate to different activities doesn't mean that you will.
- If you really want to achieve something you will need to commit to some specific time to work with your coach. Arguably the more time that you commit, the faster you will achieve your goals.

For your own health (mental & physical) I would suggest that you do not commit 100% of this time. If you are choosing to commit a high percentage of your available time to this coaching, set a specific deadline for this commitment. When the deadline occurs you can assess your progress and possibly reprioritize some other things in your life.

Decide how much time you are committing and commit it:

- Only you can determine how much time you are willing to commit here.

- This initial amount of time may stretch you but being uncomfortable for short periods isn't necessarily a bad thing.

Confirm how much time you are allocating, write it down and commit that you have allocated this time.

Exercise Fourteen   The Personality test

Whether you are going to use your test results to compare yourself to prospective coaches or just to get to know yourself better, you can reap some benefits here.

If you are choosing a test for comparison with potential coaches, determine what information you can find out about them and choose a test that you have their results for.

- Complete the relevant a personality test and compare your results with the potential coach.
- Take a note of your results and bear this in mind when you are reviewing the resources provided by potential coaches.
- If you determine that they are the same or different personalities to you then review the benefits of diversity and similarity (in this chapter) during your considerations.

If you do a quick google search you will find lots of personality tests online. Although you may have your own preferences I suggest you may want to focus on one of the more popular systems such as the "DISC" or "Wealth Dynamics" system. A more popular system may make it easier to find the corresponding information on a potential coach.

N.B.   Even if you decide to forgo this step of the analysis for a potential coach, a profile test can be a great start to your own journey of self-examination before you open yourself up to someone else's ideas.

Exercise Fifteen   **The VAK Test**

Choose a VAK test and complete it.

If you do a quick google search you will find lots of free VAK tests online, just pick one and complete the test.

- If you find that you are drawn to either an online test or a book you may already be noticing a penchant for one style over another.
- Take a note of the results and bear this in mind when you are reviewing the resources provided by potential coaches.

Exercise Sixteen   **Determine your own ethical compass**

You can choose any of the integrity or ethical tests online (or in a book).

In this exercise I want you to complete at least one online test to see where you sit on the ethical scale.

- Find a test (through an online search, the library etc.) and complete it.
- Take these results into consideration when you are judging a potential coach.
- The results will not necessarily give you total validation that you are a good or bad person.
- The purpose of taking the test is just to provide you some perspective before you start judging potential coaches.

Exercise Seventeen   **Compile your checklist**

In the next chapter we are going to start the research phase of this process so now is the time to define an initial checklist.

In this exercise you need to choose five to ten bullet points that meet the criteria relevant to the area of writing that you are seeking a coach.

- Use the examples above as guides or choose any other criteria that you deem relevant.
- Once you have determined your criteria checklist keep it handy for the next chapter.

Exercise Eighteen   **Set up your tracking system**

Now that you have seen how I keep track of my research, I want you to set up your own table or tracker. You can use whatever you are comfortable with but below are a few options:

- Open a blank spreadsheet on your computer or any other device and fill out your preferred column headings. Saving it somewhere easily accessible to you.
- Draw a table on a whiteboard and add your column headings.
- Open a blank word document and insert a table in that document with the relevant column headings. Saving it somewhere easily accessible to you.
- Open your notebook to a blank page and draw a table with the relevant column headings. Ensure that this notebook is accessible during any research.

Now that you have your tracker set up start to use it.

Exercise Nineteen　　　　　**The google search**

As I stated above, a google search is a great place to start your research. Remember that you must be specific in your search terms.

Type in your first search term and click on suitable links. Some examples for your search could be:

- "Who can help me write a novel"?
- "How do I get more book sales on amazon"?
- "How do I self-publish my book"?
- "Help me write a novel".

You will get lots of results so remain focused and if you click on a link that isn't immediately relevant, go back to your search and click on a different link.

Once you have found a relevant source, rate the coach against your initial criteria (ensuring that you populate your tracker with the information.

Complete this process until you have a short list of three to six potential coaches.

Exercise Twenty　　　　　**Further verification**

Your initial criteria should have narrowed down your potential coaches so now we start to dig a little deeper.

Choose one website or social media platform that you are comfortable with and do a search using that coach's name.

Some suggestions for this search are

- Search for their books on amazon.com.
- Search on relevant Facebook groups using their name (typing the name into the search box in that group).

- Search on Youtube and listen to their voice for a few minutes.
- Search Reddit forums for mentions of this coach.

Run this search for each of your short list of potential coaches and confirm that they still meet your initial criteria.

Exercise Twenty One   Even Further verification
If you have enough information from the previous exercise then move on and make a decision. If not work through this exercise to provide you an extra source of research verification.

Choose a second social media platform (preferably one that you are also comfortable navigating).

Carry out a further search for these coaches to confirm they still meet your criteria.

- If your potential coaches are all scoring exactly the same consider adding extra criteria.
- One way of tweaking your criteria is to reduce your budget.
- If your initial budget was $5000 and you reduce the limit to $4000, you can now determine which coach's services still fall within that budget.
- You may have looked for three references for a coach, try only choosing coaches with ten references. This should filter out some of the coaches.

Exercise Twenty Two   Make a decision
Although you can run your potential coaches through every search engine and social media platform available, at some stage you have to make a choice.

- If you can't reduce your shortlist down to one potential coach (all things being equal) just pick the one whose name comes first alphabetically.
- I honestly believe that by now there should be one coach that stands out as meeting your criteria.
- By choosing a coach by their alphabetical name you are not making a random choice but are avoiding procrastination, after your previous research.

In the next chapter we will look at how you are going to utilize this coach. While you are choosing how you will use a coach, if you determine your recent choice doesn't suit your needs, you can always revert back to this exercise.

If you have to revert back to this exercise, just choose the next coach in alphabetical order from your short list.

Exercise Twenty Three   Confirm what coach's services you will employ.
You should now have determined which coaching services are best going to suit your requirements. Taking into account all of the factors that we have covered in this book (and any extra you decided to add), you now need to focus and choose what services you want to proceed with.

- Are you going to choose to be self-reliant and just use a set course or book?
- Are you going to use a coaching system that relies on the support of a team?
- Are you going to commit to employing a one on one coach?

Decide now and Say out loud "I (insert your own name) have decided that to reach my goal of (insert your writing goal), I am committed to (insert your commitment here)".

e.g. "I Ged have decided that to reach my goal of writing and publishing my first novel, I am committed to enrolling on an online coaching course with Joanna Penn".

Exercise Twenty Four   Employ your coach
This is where the rubber meets the road. You have spent the time and effort to work through this process and I congratulate you on that. It's time to commit and connect with your resources.

From the previous exercise you have committed how you want to use a coach but perhaps you have found two coaches that provide very similar services. It's time to flip a coin.

If you truly can't choose between them then actually flip a coin and choose one as you are more than likely just procrastinating. You may be surprised that when you decide to use a coin toss to choose between two coaches, one will suddenly stand out above the other.

Do not hesitate anymore, choose your coach and then take the relevant next step:

- If you are going to follow a course from a coach's books, purchase the physical or digital versions of the books.
- If you are going to employ a one on one coach, contact the coach and notify them of your intention.
- If you are going to follow a coach's online course, get out your credit card (or Pay Pal account etc.) and enrol online now.

Appendix D   A tribute to the reader

A tribute to you the reader

I hope that you have enjoyed reading this book as much as I've enjoyed writing it.

I'm sure that if you have worked through the chapters, you now have a writing coach who meets your needs.

When I wrote my annual goals this year I included, "To help others succeed" as one of my top goals.

If you have enjoyed this book please feel free to provide feedback with a review on Amazon so that I can reach more people and help more people succeed.

About the author

Ged Cusack is a Yorkshireman (Originally from Bradford in England), currently living in New Zealand.

His has a varied background encompassing 22 years as a British military engineer, several years in post-earthquake project management, business coaching and many more ventures.

He is passionate about helping others succeed and providing as many resources as possible to make that happen.

Other titles by this author

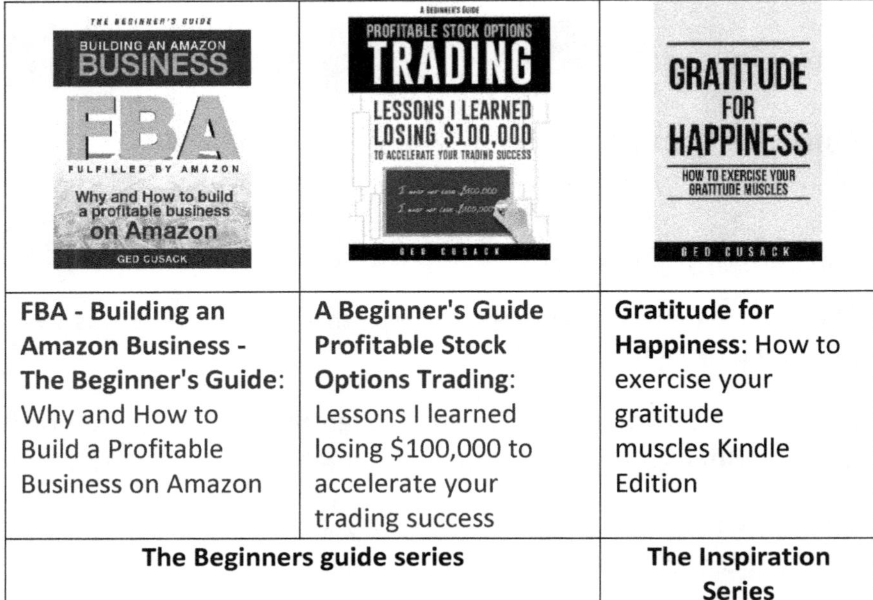

FBA - Building an Amazon Business - The Beginner's Guide: Why and How to Build a Profitable Business on Amazon	**A Beginner's Guide Profitable Stock Options Trading**: Lessons I learned losing $100,000 to accelerate your trading success	**Gratitude for Happiness**: How to exercise your gratitude muscles Kindle Edition
The Beginners guide series		**The Inspiration Series**

Free stuff

For anyone interested in building an online business, Ged has created a free online course (to help you choose the online business that suits you).

Follow this link for access to this free course http://creating-clarity-from-chaos.thinkific.com/courses/take/3-steps-to-choosing-your-profitable-online-business/

Appendix E   Some suggested resources

This book is designed to be a standalone book that provides you a process to choose the right writing coach for you.

I have purposely minimized use of hyperlinks, because I have no control over external websites and their continuity of providing resources. I have, however, provided overviews of a few useful resources and enough information that you can find them online.

I receive no financial remuneration from any of the people listed here and these suggestions are based solely on my personal experiences and research.

At the time of writing, all the resources listed here are live. Knowing that the people mentioned here provide high quality resources, if they remove these resources in the future it's likely to be because they have replaced them with something better.

Remember that there is a process in this book to choose the coach for you; not everyone listed here is suitable for every situation on your writing journey.

Alex Foster

Alex is a prolific writer and has a selection of several free ($0.00) books available, such as on Amazon.com, covering multiple aspects of the writing process. If you have a limited budget his books are a great place to start in regard to the writing process.

He has several books aimed at writing and publishing on Amazon.

Dave Chesson (The Kindlepreneur)

Dave Chesson's blog the Kindlepreneur is nothing short of magical. Although he probably doesn't class himself as a coach, he provides so much useful (free) content that he could be.

You may not employ him to teach you creative writing but when it comes to elements of writing that will help you sell your book on kindle, he ranks high on the list of teachers and providers.

Joanna Penn

Joanna is one of my favourite authors for giving back. She has some amazing free resources on her website thecreativepenn.com. Here you'll find hundreds of episodes of her podcast where she is constantly interviewing the right people who always seem to bring the right writing tools to the fore. The podcasts are also transcribed which I love as a speed reader.

As well as a plethora of fiction books she has also published lots of great nonfiction resource books for authors, including "How to make a living with your writing" and "Successful self-Publishing".

Joanna also has several coaching courses available:

- How to write a Novel: From idea to First Draft to finished Manuscript - $300
- Creative Freedom course: Learning how to make a living from your writing - $497

Jonathan Green

With his brand "serve no master" Jonathan provides a wealth of information to become a successful author. His blog and podcast (under the "serve no master" umbrella) provide up to date information on the techniques required of a successful author. He also has several books around online income, including his book "20k a day: How to launch more books and make more money".

As with Steve Scott, Jonathon's resources help you in starting a blog and many more of your future marketing activities.

Steve Scott

Steve is another prolific writer and has a selection of great guidance books available in kindle format, ranging from $0.99 - $4.99. Steve has books to help you with your book sales (such as "61 ways to sell more nonfiction kindle books" and also books on other online marketing activities.

You may not think some of his books (such as how to start a successful blog) are relevant to a book writer. It's worth noting that if you want to be a successful writer you may have to undertake activities such as blogging further in your writing career.